India's Maritime Security

Issues and Challenges

India's Maritime Security

Issues and Challenges

Dr. Sanjay Kumar
Associate Professor
Department of Defence Studies
Meerut College, Meerut

Dr. Bina Rai
Associate Professor
Department of Political Science
R.G.P.G. College, Meerut

Dr. Neelam Kumari
Associate Professor
Department of Chemistry
Meerut College, Meerut

in collaboration with
ARIDSS, Meerut

Goel Publications

New Delhi - 110002

India's Maritime Security: Issues and Challenges

First Published in 2021

₹ 650

ISBN 978-81-946884-6-4

Published by : **Goel Publications**

G-Floor, 4855/24, Ansari Road,

Daryaganj, Delhi - 110002

Tel. : 9999819813

Email: goelpublications@gmail.com

Laser Typesetting : Ankita Graphics, Delhi

Printer : GS offset, Shahdra, Delhi

Contents

Preface

The present book has made a descriptive analysis on Maritime Security Challenges of India. In the context of emerging multi-fold maritime security challenges, the study on India's maritime security holds immense significance. Maritime security represents the broadest approach to issues and aspects which pertain to the sea and have an important bearing on the country's security. Ensuring Maritime security is of utmost importance both strategically and economically given India's growing dependence on sea for overseas trade and energy security. The 26/11 Mumbai attack was an eye opener for our country in a sense that it calls upon the need to strengthen maritime power to meet the threats posed by maritime terrorism and piracy. Since then the naval forces were deployed to meet the threats in piracy affected areas.

In recent decades with the increasing awareness at the global level about the need to strengthen maritime security, the geo-strategic and geo-economic significance of Indian Ocean at the regional and global level has increased tremendously. The Indian Ocean is fast becoming the new center of economic gravity, as it ties together the economic fortunes of emerging Asia, the US, and Europe. Maritime rivalries in the Indian Ocean are an early indicator of the return of great-power politics to the limelight of the international arena.

In the 21st century, the importance of Indian Ocean has

gained immense significance resulted in competition and cooperation over the control of the Ocean. Global and regional powers interest in the whole Indian Ocean region is on the rise. The reasons for this include security concerns about instability that characterises and destabilises the region, the region's vital role in oil production and its importance for energy shipments, the wealth of resources and raw materials in the region, involvement of extra-regional powers in a number of conflicts, and the rise of new regional powers and their ability to project their power.

Today the Indian Ocean's traditional status as an international trade highway is more significant than ever before, while international military presence in the ocean is unprecedented. Given India's strategic location, its size, available mineral, agricultural, human and technological resources, it becomes imperative that New Delhi plays a befitting role in the Indian Ocean region. India will need to strengthen its activities in the Indian Ocean thereby expand its strategic influence in the region. This would also mean preventing the Ocean from being used as a platform to launch attack against the stability and security of our country. It will need to strengthen its muscles on all these fronts and its security components. Its military capability particularly naval capability needs to be strengthened by equipping them with advance weapons to guard its territorial integrity and underpin safeguarding and promoting national interests in the Indian Ocean region.

The Indian Ocean and its littoral and island states constitute geostrategic region in world politics. The whole expanse of the region is geo-strategically important as it is through this that a critical sea lines of communications (SLOCs) - for the trade and energy flow- pass. The problem of piracy disrupting the SLOCs in the two maritime choke points, one on the western end of IOR- the strait of Hormuz and one on the eastern end- the Malacca strait- complicate the geo-strategic scenario.

Although the Indian security forces had responded swiftly to '26/11 Mumbai attack', but it exposed three significant cracks in India's maritime security calculus, the porous nature of India's coastline; the inadequate surveillance of the maritime domain; and the lack of inter-agency coordination. Post the 26/11 attacks, the Indian government specially, Indian Navy undertook a number of proactive measures to restructure coastal security and push the defensive perimeter further away from the coast into the seas. Seeing the nature of maritime challenges India faced at present, naval forces such as naval warships, coast guards, marine police and commandos are being employed to ensure 'good order at sea'. The Indian Navy and the Coast Guard has a significant role to play in ensuring maritime security unilaterally or in coordination with navies of other countries. Ensuring energy security would require assessing how India responds to meet such challenges.

China's political, diplomatic and military efforts in the Indian Ocean seem to exhibit a desire to project influence vis-à-vis competing powers in the region, such as the US and India. The growing Chinese capabilities in the Indian Ocean are posing challenge to the US influence and a security challenges for India in the region. Hence, the Indian Ocean region has assumed a new importance as various powers are once again vying for the control of the waves in this part of the world. Given the China's growing reliance on imported sources of energy to sustain its economic growth at domestic level, any disruption in the Indian Ocean can have a potentially catastrophic impact for the world's economic stability and have potential to threaten security environment in the region (IOR).

Much can be gained from a cooperative regional approach between states that promotes consultation not confrontation, reassurance not deterrence, transparency not secrecy, prevention not correction, and interdependence not unilateralism. In such circumstances navies can contribute much towards enhancing maritime security, managing disasters, providing humanitarian assistance and limiting environmental security challenges. Regional cooperation can therefore be a force multiplier and is certainly desirable in the vast, relatively poorly policed Indian Ocean.

We express our gratitude to the *Indian Council for Social Science Research (ICSSR), New Delhi* for providing the grant for the research project. Without financial support from the ICSSR, this report would not have seen the light of day. The completion of this research project was made possible through the support of people whom we would like to acknowledge. We would like to acknowledge the unwavering support of Prof. Gautam Sen, Prof. Rajendra Prasad, Prof. Gopalji Malviya, Prof. Hari Saran, Prof. M.N. Varma, Lt. Gen. R.N. Singh, Lt. Gen. R.C. Chadha, Lt. Gen. J.S. Negi, Vice Admiral Ajit Kumar, Maj.Gen.O.P. Gulia, Maj. Gen. P.K. Goswami, Gp. Capt. Sharad Tiwari, Gp. Capt. (Dr.) R.K. Singh, Dr. R.S. Panday, Prof.Prashant Agarwal, Dr. Abhay Kumar Singh, Dr. Dhirendra Dwivedi, Dr. Alka Chaudhary, Dr. Bhupander Singh, Dr. Ravinder Nirwal, Dr. Neelam Kumari, Sh. Ajay Kumar Gupta, Sh. Mahesh Madhukar, Smt. Revathy Vishwanath, for their insightful suggestions in the every state of the research project. We also wish to express our thanks to Dr. Monu Kushwaha, Dr. Mohammad Samir Hussain, Dr. Ruchi Singh, Dr. Sanjay Kumar Panday, for assistance in the completion of this book in time.

Nevertheless, we also extend our heartiest thankful to the members and staff of the Library of United Service Institution, Institute of Defence and Strategic Analysis, National Maritime Foundation, Jawaharlal Nehru University, India International Centre, Observer Research Foundation, USI, ICSSR and Teen Murti libraries for extending the much-needed support while collecting the research material.

Dr. Sanjay Kumar, Dr. Bina Rai

Dr. Neelam Kumari

1

Introduction

Research seeks to make an analytical and critical study on maritime security challenges, terrorism and piracy at sea in the global era. With the global geopolitical shift in the power balances from Europe to the Indo-Pacific, the fate of the Indian Ocean has changed significantly. The Indian Ocean once regarded as a neglected Ocean has today, becomes the centre-stage of global geopolitics. It is the hub of political, strategic and economic activities due to the presence of conventional and nuclear vessels of the major powers and nuclear-weapon states such as the United States, Russia, China, France, Australia, India, etc.

The Indian Ocean can be seen as a rich and diverse physical environment, a great medium for transportation, an important theatre of military activities, a vast area of leisure, as well as an area under limited legislation and even less policing. The Indian Ocean is of vital and growing strategic importance to India as it is faced with a major challenge in gaining access to necessary energy resources. The significance of the Indian Ocean also lies in the view of its increasing role in global energy transport, but also due to the growing economic importance to India. There is an expanding gap between oil and natural gas consumption and the production of these resources resulting in the country's growing reliance on imports. In recent decades with the increasing awareness at the global level about the need to strengthen maritime security, the geo-strategic and geo-economic significance of Indian Ocean at the regional and global level has increased tremendously.

The geo-economic and geo-strategic significance of the Indian Ocean has been explored many centuries back. Since then, the Indian Ocean has seen intense maritime activity, primarily for trade. Over the centuries, the Indian Ocean has been an important international waterway.[1] Mohan Malik in his well-written book titled, China and India: Great Power Rivals has noted that 'Current geostrategic, economic, energy and demographic trends indicate that the Indian Ocean Region (IOR), could well emerge as the strategic centre of the twenty-first century, much as the Atlantic and Pacific oceans played this role in the twentieth century.'[2] The Indian Ocean has always had a major share of global piracy and terror attacks among other illegal activities in territorial waters due to weak maritime policing. From whichever direction, the entry into the Indian Ocean is constrained by geographic imperatives, thus making the Indian Ocean seem bereft of any collective maritime security arrangements. From the national security point of view, Indian Ocean holds immense significance for our country. India's pioneer geo-politician, K.M. Panikkar, has pointed out many decades back that since India's future was dependent on the Indian Ocean, then 'the Indian Ocean must therefore remain truly Indian'. Further, he pointed out: 'A true appreciation of Indian historical forces will show beyond doubt, that whoever controls the Indian Ocean has India at its mercy.'[3] While A.T. Mahan had once opined that, 'Whoever controls the Indian Ocean dominates Asia. This ocean is the key to the seven seas in the twenty-first century, the destiny of the world will be decided in these waters.'[4]

India's continued economic development is dependent

on secure routes for energy supplies and the movement of its trade through the Indian Ocean region. The very geostrategic location of the Indian Ocean has without any doubt attracted the attention of both regional and global powers, seeking to expand their influence in the ocean. In the Heartland Theory as propounded by Halford J. Mackinder, the Indian Ocean occupies a significant place in the outer or Insular Crescent just down south of the Inner or Marginal Crescent surrounding the Pivot Area.[5]

The Indian Ocean is one of the great oceans which are surrounded by the continents of Asia, Africa and Australia. It is separated from the Antarctic continent by the Antarctic Circle. It is the smallest of the three big Oceans, covering an Oceanic area of nearly 75 million square kilometres. Unlike the Atlantic and Pacific Oceans, it does not cover the temperate zone of the northern hemisphere. The greatest depth of the Indian Ocean is over 24,000 feet in the Java Trench, and the average depth of 13,000 far exceeds that of the Atlantic Ocean. The Indus, Ganges, Irrawaddy, Tigris-Euphrates, Zambezi and Limpopo are the large rivers emptying into the Indian Ocean. The Arabian Sea and the Bay of Bengal are its two major arms.[6]

The Indian Ocean occupies 20 per cent of the world's oceanic surface. It has a number of sea bodies, important islands and international ports. Forty-seven countries have the Indian Ocean on their shores. This ocean includes the Andaman Sea, Arabian Sea, Bay of Bengal, Flores Sea, Great Australian Bight, Gulf of Aden, Gulf of Mannar, Laccadive Sea, Gulf of Oman, Java Sea, Mozambique Channel, Persian Gulf, Red Sea, Savu Sea, Strait of Malacca, and the Timor Sea. In its geographical contexts, the Indian Ocean is linked with the Pacific Ocean through the South China Sea and the East China Sea. This brings into context the Indo-Pacific geographical prism that ties the Asian landmass on both oceanic rimlands. While, the islands of significance in this ocean include the Coco Islands, Andaman Islands, Sri Lanka, Maldives, Diego Garcia, Seychelles and Mauritius. The Ocean also has major seaports like Chittagong in Bangladesh; Trincomalee, Colombo and (Hambantota - planned) in Sri Lanka; Freemantle in Western Australia; Vishakhapatnam, Cochin, Karwar in India; Gwadar and Ormara in Pakistan; Port Louis in Mauritius; Port Victoria in Seychelles; and Phuket in Thailand.[7]

The Indian Ocean has for the last many decades remained an area of strategic competition. One of the key reason for this can be reflected from the fact that in the north-western corner is located in the principal world source of surplus oil. Besides, it includes major highways of international commerce and the essential maritime route between the eastern and western parts of the erstwhile Soviet Union.

India's new economic policy and its quest for energy security have helped to rapidly expand India's economic links in the IOR region. Besides rising India's weight in the region, they also have provided depth to India's overall political relations in the IOR. As India's economic and political stakes in the IOR region began to grow, there has been a perceptible impact on India's security policy towards the Indian Ocean region. The key challenge ahead of India in the coming years of the 21st century would be in terms of maintaining a secure strategic position in the Indian Ocean region. The main argument of the present study is that for India to realise its economic and strategic potential, it will need to give due importance to the Indian Ocean by building adequate infrastructure and evolving a national consensus on the usage of the seas. Further, it argues that India's desired role of being the net provider of security in the IOR can only be sustained by strengthening its maritime capability.

Map 1.1 : The Indian Ocean Area

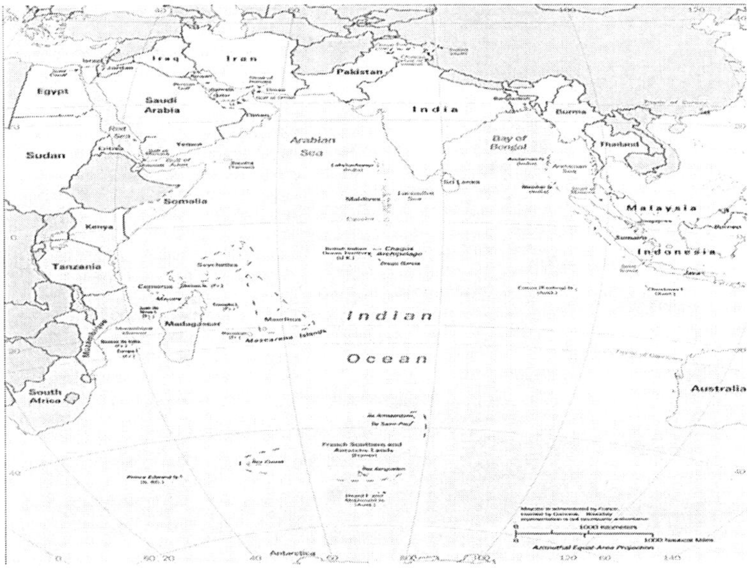

Source: Perry-Castañeda Library Map Collection: 'Indian Ocean Maps', the University of Texas at Austin, available at *<http:/ /www.lib.utexas.edu/maps/islands_oceans_poles/indianoceanarea. jpg>*.

Statement of the Problem

The 21st century has witnessed a strategic reassessment of the geo-strategic and geo-economic significance of the Indian Ocean. Renowned strategic thinker, Robert Kaplan has opined that the Indian Ocean is an area that has become witness to knock for power and subsequent shifts in the dynamics of the region. It is a very active Ocean, perceived by many as the emerging centre of gravity in the strategic world. Its activities in the region are defined by extensive trade, energy transfers and a spectrum that ranges from political turbulence on one end, to threats from piracy, terrorism and transnational crime on the other.[8]

There emerged a growing competition between Indian Ocean states for power and influence within the region. While this competition for influence is inextricably linked to competition for resources, other geostrategic motives may also be significant, particularly as leading states such as India and China seek to balance against each other and smaller states choose to bandwagon with one or both for security. India, in particular, has developed a substantial interest in the stability of the Indian Ocean region as a whole. Ensuring access to the Indian Ocean will require a more integrated approach to the region.

From India's geo-strategic viewpoint, the Indian Ocean may be subdivided into four major zones: one, the Bay of Bengal region and neighbourhood; two, the Central Indian Ocean region; three, the Arabian Sea and its natural extensions; and four, the West Indian Ocean region. Each of these zones offers India an array of interests as well as challenges. It is being argued that 'India-like other states that are geographically large and also ambitious-believes that its security will be best guaranteed by enlarging its security perimeter and, specifically, achieving a position of influence in the larger region that encompasses the Indian Ocean. New Delhi regards the Indian Ocean as its backyard and deems it both natural and desirable that India function as, eventually, the leader and the predominant influence in this region.'[9]

The Indian Ocean is considered one of the world's busiest international trade corridors due to the expansion of Asian economies and the increased need for raw materials and energy resources from the Middle East and Africa. The global economy is built on the integrated supply chain which is greatly supported by the maritime environment making the Indian Ocean an important highway of commerce, with significant geostrategic and geo-economic value in the global scene.

Since the main mode of transportation of goods and petroleum products across the world is done through the sea, therefore maritime security of the Indian Ocean assumes immense significance to all states. With almost 90 per cent of the consumer goods and 65 per cent of the petroleum products carried on seas. The Indian Ocean accounts for half of the world's container traffic, whereas over 70 per cent of the total traffic of petroleum products passes through the Indian Ocean, on its way from the Middle East to the Pacific.[10] Maritime security has been and continues to be a topic of discussion in the international arena as most of the world's trade including oil transport takes place in the Indian Ocean waters. The discussions and debates revolve around the degree of importance of the Indian Ocean to the states within the region and those that are directly and indirectly impacted by the activities in the Indian Ocean. The international community has continued to witness transnational challenges which range from the trafficking of arms, drugs, humans, contraband; international terrorism, oil theft or bunkering, piracy, poaching (fish), illegal mining, pollution through illegal dumping of solid and hazardous waste.

As globalization intensifies and the need for oil globally increases, states along the Indian Ocean are being faced with a security problem that is directly linked with activities across the sea. This has led to such states facing the challenge of adjusting to the unstable environment, with peace being an objective yet to be achieved. Several states and other non-state actors have sought consolidated and comprehensive approaches to effective maritime policy; however, they have given very little attention to the need to understand the peace and stability component of the maritime environment. Bearing in mind the importance of the Indian Ocean to the transport of the energy resources and commodities, as well as the importance of these maritime lines in the drug trafficking, piracy and even terrorism, India will continue its monitoring and control policy in the region. Given its geostrategic location, India cannot remain oblivious to developments taking place in the Indian Ocean as it directly impinges on its security and prosperity.

Geographical and Strategic Dimension of Indian Ocean

Bound by landmasses on three sides, the Indian Ocean

has some unique features. These include the absence of seas beyond 25°N, while land areas south of 10°S exist only in Africa, Australia and Antarctica.[11] The Indian Ocean occupies a vast region. It spreads over seven sub-regions (Southern Africa, Eastern Africa and the Horn, the Gulf littoral and Arabian Peninsula, South Asia, South East Asia, Australia and the Indian Ocean Islands) and embraces 33 countries.[12] Its western border is continental Africa to a longitude of 20° E, where it stretches south from Cape Agulhas; its northern border is continental Asia from Suez to the Malay Peninsula; in the east, it incorporates Singapore, the Indonesian archipelago, Australia to longitude 147° E and Tasmania; while in the south it stretches to latitude 60° S as determined per the Antarctic Treaty of 1959.[13]

Map 1.2 : Topographic-Bathymetric Map of the Indian Ocean

Source: Carlo Masala, et. al., "Maritime Security in the Indian Ocean- For Greater German Engagement in the Ocean of the 21st Century", *Konrad Adenauer Stiftung*, No. 172, June 2015, p. 2.

Table 1.1 : The 51 States of the Indian Ocean Region

Indian Ocean rim states		Other coastal states of the Red Sea and the Persian Gulf	Indian Ocean land-locked states
Australia	Mozambique	Bahrain	Afghanistan
Bangladesh	Oman	Egypt	Bhutan
Burma (Myanmar)	Pakistan	Eritrea	Botswana
Comoros	Seychelles	Iraq	Burundi
Djibouti	Singapore	Israel	Ethiopia
France*	Somalia	Jordan	Lesotho
Kenya	South Africa	Kuwait	Malawi
India	Sri Lanka	Qatar	Nepal
Indonesia	Tanzania	Saudi Arabia	Rwanda
Iran	Thailand	Sudan	Swaziland
Madagascar	Timor-Leste		Uganda
Malaysia	United Arab Emirates		Zambia
Maldives			Zimbabwe
Mauritius	United Kingdom*		
	Yemen		

Source: Dennis Rumley (ed.), *The Indian Ocean Region: Security, Stability and Sustainability in the 21st Century* (Australia India Institute, 2013), p. 31.

There are a total of 51 states, 28 of which are Indian Ocean rim states, plus further 10 that are coastal states of the Red Sea and the Persian Gulf, together with an additional 13 Indian Ocean land-locked states (for details refer to table 1.1). The Indian Ocean is of particular importance owing to its geographical structure wherein most of its area is walled off on three sides by land and the southern side of Asia forms the roof above. However, it is the Indian subcontinent jutting out far into the sea which changes the character of the Indian Ocean and differentiates it from the Pacific and the Atlantic.[14] From the geographical point of view, it is situated between the Atlantic and the Pacific Ocean, thereby serving as a natural 'transit lounge' for most of the traffic from the Atlantic to the Pacific and vice versa. One of the characteristic features that distinguish the Indian Ocean from the Atlantic and the Pacific as 'open' oceans is that the Indian Ocean can only be accessed through several choke points: From the West via Cape of Good Hope and the Straits of Madagascar, from the North via the Bab el-Mandeb at the end of the Red Sea and the Straits of Hormuz at the exit of the Persian Gulf, from the East via the Straits of Malacca, the Sunda and Lombok-Straits and the Ombai-Wetar-Straits.[15]

The Indian Ocean, the third largest of the world oceans, is unique with respect to its shape, size and its strategic location. Unlike the Atlantic and the Pacific Ocean; the Indian Ocean waters do not intermingle with those of the Arctic Ocean. Since the vast solid Eurasian landmass lies to its north, blocking its reach to the Arctic waters. Of course, like the other two larger Oceans, the Indian Ocean waters mix up with those of the Antarctic Ocean.[16]

Figure 1.1 : Geo-Strategic Significance of Indian Ocean

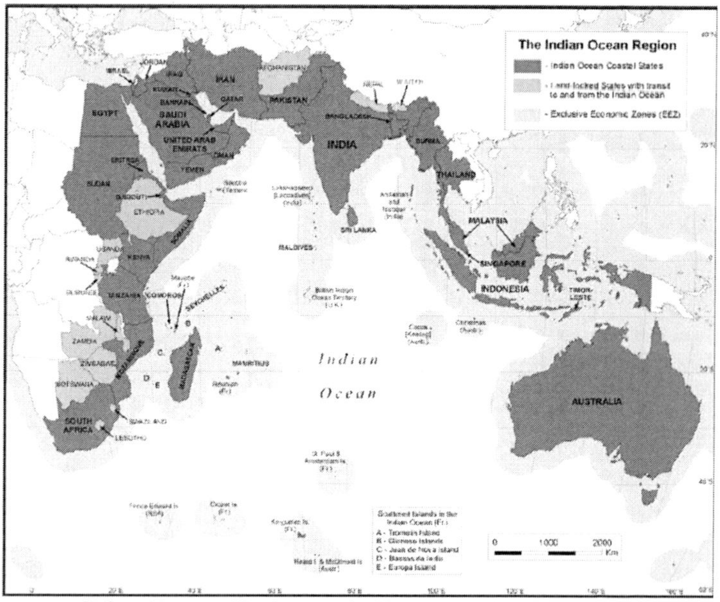

Source: Sidra Tariq, "India and China in the Indian Ocean: A Complex Interplay of Geopolitics", *Institute of Regional Studies*, Islamabad, January-February 2014, p. 3.

From the geostrategic point of view, the Indian Ocean is unique in the sense that it is closed to the north by the Eurasian continent and that maritime communication to the outside world is mostly constrained by a small number of chokepoints. Known for being the third-largest Ocean in the world, the Indian Ocean is being neighbored to Asia in its north, Africa to its west, Indo-China to its east while Antarctica lies in its south. It ranges from north to south from the Bay of Bengal to Antarctica with an estimated area of 9600 kilometres, while it extends from west to east from Southern Africa to Western Australia with the range of 7800 kilometres. It covers almost 20 per cent of the world's water. Its total area is about 68.556 million square kilometre and it is almost 5.5 times larger than the United States. The ocean total area includes Andaman Sea, Arabian Sea, Bay of Bengal, Flores Sea, Great Australian Bight, Gulf of Aden, Gulf of Oman, Java Sea, Mozambique Channel, Persian Gulf, Red Sea, Savu Sea, Strait of Malacca, Timor Sea, and other tributary water bodies.[17]

Figure 1.2 : Indian Ocean: Littoral and Island States

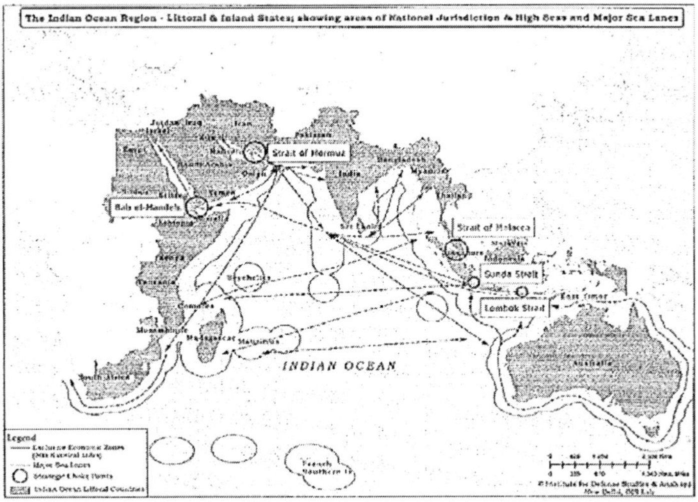

Source: Lee Cordner, "National Security Interests and the Indian Ocean: An Australian Perspective", *Rumlae Research Paper,* No. 16-16, Adelaide Law School, The University of Adelaide, 2016, p. 2.

The Arabian Sea, with its Red Sea, Persian Gulf and the Hormuz and Tirana Straits; the Bay of Bengal, the Andaman Sea, the Mozambique Channel, etc, make the total oceanic area of the Indian Ocean around 2.5 million square km; which is roughly equal to the combined area of the Asian and African continents. The oceanic depth varies from 1793 m in the north Arabian Sea, and 2400 m in the Kerguelen Plateau to 7010 m in Sunda Trench. The Indian Ocean islands are irregular in distribution and origin, and the basin formation by the mid-Oceanic ridge is similar to that of the Atlantic Ocean but is shorter and wider.[18]

The principal topographical characteristic of the Indian Ocean is that it is divided into two basins, like the Atlantic by a mid-oceanic ridge. The Indian Ocean deep waters are thus divided into three large troughs by the mid-oceanic Ridge: (1) the North-East, the Central Indian and other small basins around Malagasy (2) the Southern Trough consists of the South-West Indian Ocean Basin divided by the Crozet and Kergucleau Ridges from the Indian-Antarctic Basins; and (3) the Wharton Basin is near the Sunda Trench. Other basins in the eastern trough are the Andaman and Cocos-Keeling Basins.[19]

Figure 1.3 : Indian Ocean Sea Lanes of Communications and the Key Choke Points

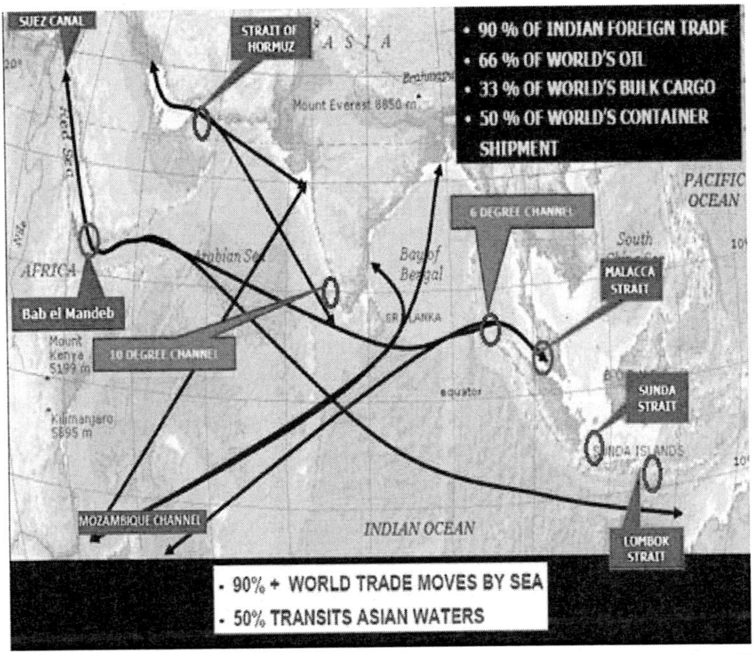

Source: *http://www.rsis.edu.sg/research/PDF/emerge_maritime_security.pdf*

From the strategic point of view, the importance of the Indian Ocean can be reflected from the fact that it is home for more than 2 billion people. It forms a vital part of the global shipping routes and network, including vital choke points. Oil from IOR remains vital today and will become more so in the foreseeable future. It provides an avenue for Great Power projection. It allows great powers to project "autonomous" military power in a very strategic area. Security and stability concerns in the region are increasing as is the prospect of conflict.[20]

The vital global shipping routes and maritime chokepoints of Indian Ocean are Strait of Hormuz, Strait of Malacca, Bab-el-Mandeb, The Sunda and Lombok straits, Mozambique Channel and Ten Degree and Six Degree

Channels (as can be seen in figure 1.3). Of these, the Suez Canal, Bab-el-Mandab and Strait of Hormuz in the north-west, the Mozambique Channel in the south-west; and Malacca Strait, Sunda Strait and Lombok Strait in the south-east of the ocean. These chokepoints typically have the potential of the sort of 'controlling' the entering and exiting flow of maritime traffic in the Indian Ocean. Of these, the more significant ones are the Suez Canal, Bab-el-Mandab, and Strait of Hormuz; and Malacca Strait.

From an economic point of view, the Indian Ocean assumes immense significance. The Ocean is rich in energy and minerals resources, both onshore and, of increasing importance, in the seabed. It is the focus of major shipping routes that provide critical links between the Atlantic and Pacific Oceans. About 30 per cent of world trade is handled in the ports of the Indian Ocean. The Indian Ocean accounts for almost 50 per cent of the world's oil production. It is estimated that around 55 per cent of known oil reserves and 40 per cent of gas reserves are in the Indian Ocean region. Half of the world's container traffic passes through the Indian Ocean. Continental shelves cover about 4.2 per cent of the total area of the Ocean and are reported to be very rich in minerals including tin, gold, uranium, cobalt, nickel, aluminium and cadmium although these resources have been largely not exploited, so far. 40 out of 54 types of raw materials used by U.S. industry are supplied by the Indian Ocean. Several of the world's top container ports, including Port Kelang and Singapore, are located in the Indian Ocean as well as some of the world's fastest-growing and busiest ports. The Ocean possesses some of the world's largest fishing grounds, providing approximately 15 per cent of the total world's fish catch (approximately 9 million tons per annum).[21]

Figure 1.4
Oil Flows through Major Chokepoints of the Indian Ocean for the Year 2003

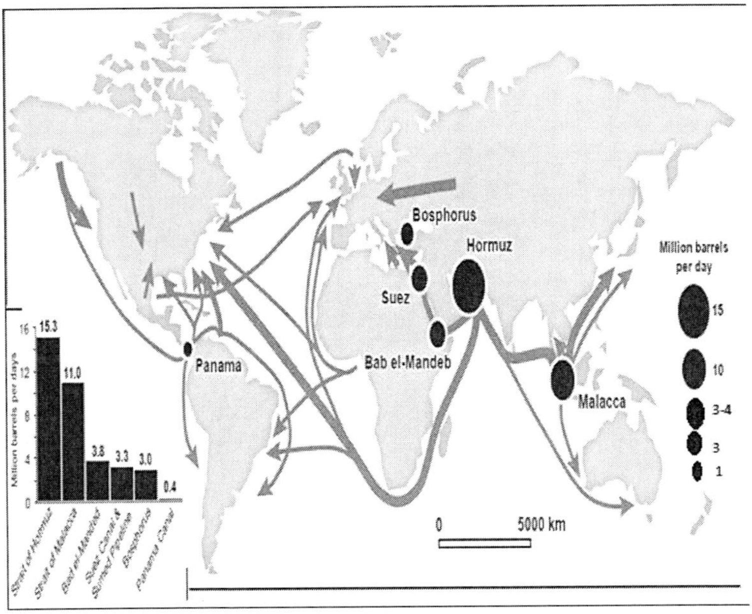

Source: Rodrigue, J., "Straits, Passages and Chokepoints a Maritime Geo-Strategy of Petroleum Distribution", *Cahiers de Géographie du Québec,* 48(135), 2004.

Key Choke Points of the Indian Ocean

Access to the Indian Ocean can be controlled by several choke points, through which much of the world's commerce flows. Nine important passages provide access into the Indian Ocean, of which five are key energy Sea Lines of Communications (SLOC). Choking any one of them would cause disruption of seaborne trade, and uncontrolled volatility in oil and commodity prices, leading to upheavals in the global economy. The Ocean and its affiliated seas hold the world's most important chokepoints for energy supply (as can be seen in Table 1.2). The major choke points of the

Indian Ocean[1] are as under:-

Table 1.2

The volume of Crude Oil and Petroleum Products Transported Through World Chokepoints, 2007-2011

Key Chokepoints	Year				
	2007	2008	2009	2010	2011
Bab-el-Mandeb Strait	4.6	4.5	2.9	2.7	3.4
Strait of Hormuz	16.7	17.5	15.7	15.9	17.0
Suez Crude Oil	1.3	1.2	0.6	0.7	0.8
Suez Petroleum Products	1.1	1.3	1.3	1.3	1.4

Notes: All estimates are in million barrels per day.

Source: Sarwar Jahan Chowdhury, "Piracy and Trafficking: Maritime and Security Policy Challenges", in Conference Proceedings on *'Major Powers' Interests in the Indian Ocean: Challenges and Options for Pakistan,* organized by the Islamabad Policy Research Institute (IPRI) and the Hanns Seidel Foundation, (HSF), Islamabad, 18-19 November 2014,p. 40.

The Strait of Hormuz: Hormuz Strait is undoubtedly the world's most strategic chokepoint with around 17 billion barrels transiting through this strait every day. Connecting the Arabian Sea to the Gulf of Oman and the Persian Gulf, it has channels 2 nautical miles (nm) wide for both inward and outbound traffic with a 2 nm wide buffer zone in between. Closure of this strait would require the use of alternative pipeline routes at increased transportation costs. However, much of the vulnerability for consumers has been reduced by two giant pipelines to Yanbu, which provide off-take in the Red Sea.

Figure 1.5

Strait of Hormuz

Source: Available at <*http://www.worldatlas.com/aatlas/infopage/hormuz.htm*>.

The Suez Canal and the Red Sea. The Suez Canal is the gateway between Europe and Asia. It is 105.4 nm long and, being entirely at sea level, does not require any locks for its operation. Closure of the Suez Canal would cause traffic to be diverted around the Cape of Good Hope, thereby increasing the transit time and transportation costs.

Figure 1.6

Suez Canal

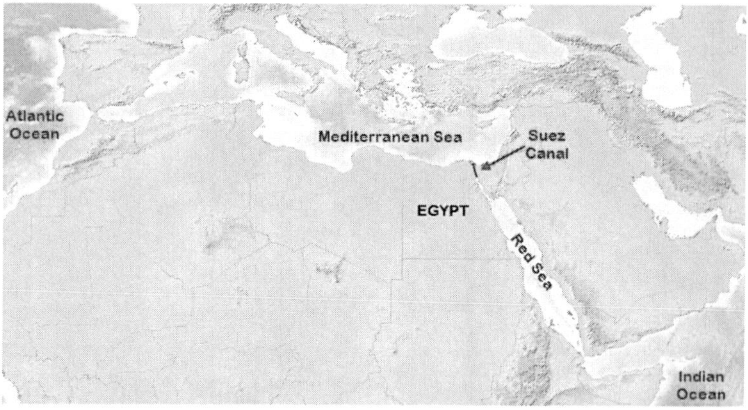

Source: Available at <*http://www.eoearth.org/view/article/156309/*>.

The Strait of Bab-el-Mandeb and Horn of Africa. The Bab-el-Mandeb connects the Gulf of Aden and the Red Sea. Closure of the Babel-Mandeb would keep tankers loaded in the Persian Gulf from reaching the Suez Canal or the Sumed Pipeline, forcing them to round the southern tip of Africa instead. This would add greatly to transit time and cost, and effectively tie-up spare tanker capacity.

The Malacca Strait: The Malacca Strait is the primary route, through which more than 50,000 vessels transit annually.[1] It represents a key chokepoint between the Indian and Pacific Oceans, forms a focus of India's maritime security plan in the northeast Indian Ocean. The Strait is one of the world's busiest waterways and constitutes a crucial trade route between East Asia, Europe and the Middle East. The Strait is largely within the territorial waters of Singapore, Indonesia and Malaysia.[2] Being on the shortest sea route connecting the Persian Gulf with East Asia and the USA, it is a critical chokepoint in the IOR. At its narrowest point, in the Philip Channel, the Malacca Strait is only 1.5 nm wide.

This creates a natural bottleneck, with potential for blockage in case of collision or grounding of ships. Closure of the strait would entail rerouting of nearly half the world's fleet, generating a requirement for additional vessel capacity and resulting in an immediate increase in worldwide freight costs. The possibility of tanker accidents in this narrow strait also raises the spectre of oil spills and widespread pollution.

Figure 1.7

Malacca, Lombok and Sunda Strait(Footnotes)

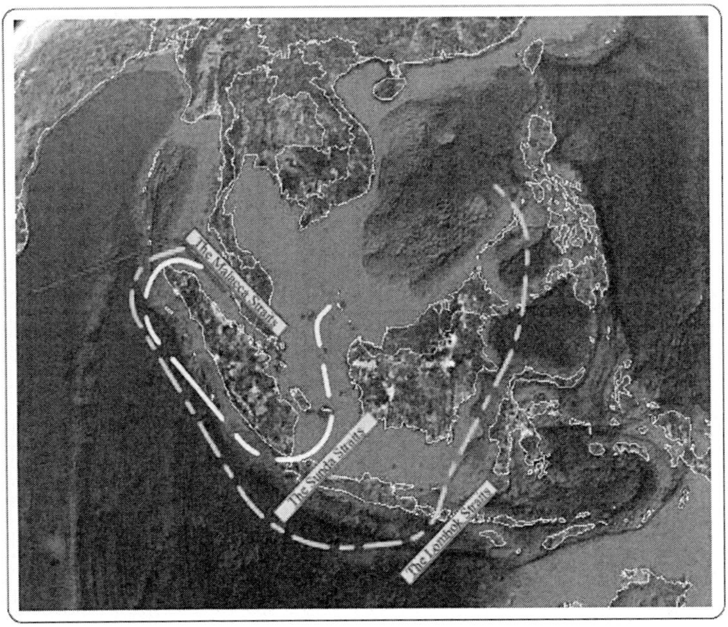

The Lombok Strait. At a minimum channel width of 11.5 nm, the Lombok Strait has sufficient width and depth and is far less congested than the Malacca Strait. Ships too large for the Strait of Malacca use this passage.

The Sunda Strait. An alternate route to the Malacca and Lombok Straits is the Sunda Strait, which is 50 nm long and 15 nm wide at its northeast entrance. Large ships avoid passage through this strait due to depth restrictions and strong currents.

The Six Degree Channel. The primary passage through the Andaman and Nicobar Islands to the Strait of Malacca is through the Six Degree Channel or Great Channel. Stretching from Indira Point on Great Nicobar to the northern tip of Aceh on the Indonesian island of Sumatra, it is an easy and wide passage without any depth limitations.

The Nine Degree Channel. The Nine Degree Channel is the most direct route through India's Lakshadweep Islands for ships sailing from the Persian Gulf bound for East Asia.

The Cape of Good Hope. The Cape of Good Hope is not a conventional choke point since the adequate depth of water lies to its south and the passage of ships is not restricted by land. However, economic sense and unfavourable currents demand that ships pass close to land, which makes them susceptible to attack and grounding.

Resource-Rich Indian Ocean

The Indian Ocean region comprises of one of the richest natural resources zones in terms of oil and mineral wealth. The ocean is rich in natural resources and its geographical space contains 62 per cent of the world's proven oil reserves, 35 per cent of world gas reserves, 40 per cent of its gold, 60 per cent of its uranium, and 80 per cent of all diamond deposits and a large variety of other mineral substances.[1] Sizable deposits of other resources are also available in the littoral areas such as uranium, tin, iron, titanium, chromite, lithium, bauxite, cobalt, nickel, manganese, rubber, gold and diamonds and accentuate the factors beckoning the attention of out-side maritime powers to the region.

Most importantly, the Indian Ocean is also a transit zone for much of the world's energy resources. In the present time, the Indian Ocean is the world's busiest trade routes connecting the Middle East, South Asia and the Asia-Pacific which has made it one vast - choke point. The seaborne oil trade is around 40 per cent of the world which goes through the Gulfs of Aden and Oman and also cross other world commerce's main chokepoints: Bab-el- Mandeb and the Straits of Hormuz and Malacca. Moreover, approximately 80 per cent of the world's seaborne trade in oil (equivalent to about one-fifth of global energy supply) - oil which fuels the economies of the United States, Japan, China and India, depends on transit shipments of Middle East oil, natural gas, and raw materials.[2] Moreover, economic and commercial growth in both the developed and developing world depends on uninterrupted access to the Indian Ocean littoral's oil and mineral resources and the goods that transit through it and particularly because 80 per cent of the trade conducted across the Indian Ocean is extra-regional.[22]

The Indian Ocean is also known for the presence of fish in large quantity. Fish production in the Indian Ocean has increased drastically from 861,000 tons in 1950 to 11.3 million tons in 2010. Unlike the other oceans in the world, Indian Oceans have the potential to sustain increased fish production. The countries of the East Indian Ocean represent a significant proportion of world fisheries, although most commercial and artisanal activity takes place in coastal zones rather than in deep water. The East Indian Ocean is home to 45 per cent of the world's fishers and brings in catches of 7 million tons of fish per year, or 8 per cent of total world fish production. While the West Indian Ocean is also characterized by overfishing and growing exploitation of deepwater fisheries. From 2000 to 2001 alone, total catches increased by 2.2 per cent, representing a 10.6 per cent increase over the previous decade.[23] For these reasons, the region has assumed tremendous strategic significance. Indeed, Robert Kaplan argues that the Indian Ocean is a key geographic space which melds energy, commerce, and security.[24]

The total oil and gas reserves held by IOR states as a percentage of the entire world's proven reserves are impressive: IOR states have more than 58 per cent of the world's proven reserves and more than 46 per cent of gas reserves. When one considers these facts and the inescapable importance of the SLOCs in the Indian Ocean connecting Asia, Europe, and Africa for the conveyance of petroleum, the significance of the IOR to the rest of the world is startling.[25]

Objectives of the Study

The study has the following objectives:-

a. To examine Socio-economic, demographic and strategic characteristics of the people and their relationship with Maritime security, terrorism and piracy at sea in the study area.

b. To analyze the factors responsible for success /failure related to the Maritime threats to India's security such as piracy, hijacking, drugs, human and small arms trafficking, Maritime terrorism and illegal migration and their impact on Maritime security challenges.

c. To investigate ongoing Maritime security challenges in India and their relationship with maritime security capabilities under several interrelated heads such as subsurface warfare, naval air armament, surface combatant amphibious and projection capabilities.

d. To study the linkages between external factors as well as internal factors and their consequences on Maritime security challenges to India in terms of terrorism and piracy at sea.

e. To evaluate the governmental role for formulating a strategic plan to get optimum benefits in the Maritime security challenges.

f. To suggests appropriate yardsticks for further strengthening the strategic plan and policies keeping in view the globalization for formulating maritime security strategies.

Research Questions

This study seeks to answer the following questions:

a. What are Maritime interest, ambitions and the key rationale behind India's emerging Maritime power?

b. How threatening are the challenges of maritime threats particularly piracy and maritime terrorism to India's maritime security?

c. Is Maritime terrorism and piracy adversely affecting economic activities in terms of trade availability due to fraud, stolen cargo and delayed trips etc.?

d. Why has Maritime security been changing in terms of security capabilities under various inter subheads like sub-surface warfare, Naval armament, surface combatant amphibious and projection capabilities?

e. What are India's policy options and responses towards maritime security challenges in the 21st century?

Hypothesis of the Study

The study is based on the following Hypothesis. They include:

a. Maritime terrorism and piracy has also a direct economic impact in terms of fraud, stolen cargos, and delayed trips, and could potentially undermine India's maritime trading ability.

b. Maritime security in the IOR in the short-to-medium term is going to be founded upon the robust and sustained naval presence of India in cooperation with other maritime countries in Asia.

c. The nature and credibility of Indian responses to maritime security challenges will depend upon its overall maritime security capability.

d. Maritime security due to environment has been changing in terms of security capability under several inter-related heads such as subsurface warfare, naval air armament, and surface combatant amphibious warfare and projection capabilities.

Outline of the Study

The present research work has been structured into five chapters including the introduction and concluding remarks that address the key aspect of the geo-economic and geo-strategic importance of the Indian Ocean for India and Maritime security challenges.

Research Methodology

The present research proposes to employ the descriptive-analytical method. It is a method in which the researcher has attempted to analyze and interpret both the primary and secondary sources. This qualitative study will seek to analyse the geo-economic and geo-strategic significance for India and the policy options for India.

The Primary sources that reveal a country's maritime security interests and strategy are normally unattainable, but some countries have implemented systems to selectively declassify official documents in order to provide justification for its policy decisions. India has never implemented a system of declassification of its official documents, but since making a more complete democratic transition, it has been more transparent in the release of annual reports, which do reveal some of its strategic preferences. For primary sources which reveal India's perceived threats and national interests, I have investigated official policy documents and speeches available via India's official government websites. The Primary Data include government officials, policymakers and planners.

For secondary sources which reveal the Indian maritime threats and national interests, I will investigate the works of leading academic scholars and journalists which scrutinize government policies and are available in numerous publicly available in the form of books, articles in journals and periodicals, reports, websites, etc. The data for the secondary sources will be collected from the various Universities, Research Centre and Institutes across India such as Jawaharlal Nehru University, Jamia Milia Islamia University, Institute for Defence Studies and Analyses, United Service Institute library, National Maritime Foundation, Indian Council of World Affairs, Library of Parliament House, Library of Indian Council of Social Science Research, External Affairs Library, National Maritime Foundation, and so on.

Review of Literatures

The useful literature for this research work is books and articles in journals and periodicals written with varying degrees of relevance on the Indian Ocean, its geo-economic, geostrategic significance for India and the emerging challenges of piracy threats and maritime terrorism and the presence of extra-regional powers in the Ocean. Thus, the books and articles would be materials that are related to the geostrategic and geo-economic significance of the India Ocean and the emerging challenges in the Ocean. Scholarly works have also been forthcoming on India's maritime interests in the Indian Ocean and its approach towards ensuring maritime security in the Ocean. Yet, not much comprehensive literary work is available which studies the threat posed by terrorism and piracy to maritime security and interests.

Manickam Venkataraman (2016), '*Piracy off the Coast of Somalia: Implications for China's Maritime Security*'[26] makes a descriptive analysis of the threats posed by piracy off the coast of Somalia. At first, it provides the conceptual note on piracy and maritime security. It discusses the background of Somalia and its failed status and brings out a short glimpse of Somalia piracy and its method of operation. China in particular has played a stringent role with regard to the piracy issue by way of cooperating with the multinational task force to combating piracy and simultaneously taking steps to adopt a comprehensive approach to maritime security.

Sam Bateman (2016) in his paper titled, *Maritime Security Governance in the Indian Ocean Region'*[27] calls for making arrangements for providing maritime security in the Indian Ocean Region (IOR) at both the national and regional levels. The main requirement at the regional level is a mechanism or mechanisms for cooperation on maritime security concerns both between regional countries themselves and between these countries and the extra-regional countries that have a legitimate interest in IOR maritime security. At a national level, the necessary capacity for providing maritime security includes arrangements for coordination between the various agencies involved and the operational capabilities for maritime law enforcement to provide good order at sea. The paper discusses the relative attributes of a navy or a coast guard to provide these capabilities. It concludes with ideas about how maritime security governance in the IOR might be improved.

Sharifah M. Alatas (2015) paper, *'India's Maritime Strategy in the Indian Ocean Region: Issues of Strategic Culture'*[28] analyses India's maritime strategy from the Cold War end to the present scenario. The author holds the view that India does have a strategic culture, but it is in its infancy. It first defines strategic culture and India's grand strategic paradigm. It also gives a brief glance on India's maritime doctrine which is designed to meet the sea-borne threats in the changing maritime security paradigm. Rising hegemonies in the IOR, mainly the US and China have prompted India to coordinate with other countries in the IOR that are equally affected by such developments. India should focus on improving relations with India's South Asia neighbours.

Eryan Ramadhani (2015) in his article titled, *China in*

the Indian Ocean Region: The Confined 'Far-Seas Operation'[29] examines China's ever-increasing interests in the Indian Ocean Region. Being relatively a newcomer to the Indian Ocean vicinity, China's interests has been to secure international shipping lanes (ISLs) and the sea lanes of communication (SLOCs) without relying too much on other players. China being the second-largest oil importer after the US is increasingly concerned about the security of the Indian Ocean. Since about 90 per cent of China's oil imports from the Middle East and Africa have to cross the Indian Ocean. For which China has embarked on Naval modernisation and has developed overseas naval bases.

P. K. Ghosh (2015) in his article titled, *Evolving Indian Ocean Governance Architecture: An Indian Perspective*[30] suggests methodologies to infuse energy into existing multilateral constructs and make them relevant towards better sea governance rather than create superfluous newer ones which are often impractical. The vast Indian Ocean is an active oceanic body encompassing extensive seaborne trade/ commerce and energy transfers. Unfortunately, it is also a region plagued with a plenitude of military, economic, religious and racial insecurities and asymmetric maritime threats. However, the common thread that binds the littorals is that most of the regional trade is seaborne and hence it forms one of the primary drivers of the economy in the region. In this context, a unified approach towards sea governance for overcoming myriad maritime threats and challenges facing the littorals is a diminished factor. The reason being that is the current maritime security architecture in the region and the various fora that uphold the same are mostly listless and in dire need of impetus. Comparatively, bi/multilateral naval engagements have been more successful. Multilateral exercises like the MILAN and IBSAMAR (as a maritime extension of IBSA) have ensured a degree of inter-operability and helped in the maintenance of "good order at sea". But these naval engagements suffer from inherent lacunae and cannot be substituted for a formal forum. The issue of sea governance is far larger than bi/multilateral naval meets and requires holistic approaches that may be missing from such naval exercises.

Pankaj K. Jha (2015) has in his work titled, *Mineral Explorations in the Indian Ocean: India's Policy Response*[31] explores India's policy response towards the mineral exploration in the Indian Ocean. India's lack of a concrete policy towards exploration for mineral resources in high seas and offshore areas has played a role, though to a limited extent, in the exploration projects being awarded to countries like Korea and China in the Indian Ocean. In 2011, China was awarded a large area in the Indian Ocean for mineral exploration. India has thence awakened to the issue and has made amends to its bureaucratic inertia. However, the question is whether these mineral exploration projects and demarcated ocean areas have economic implications only, or have larger strategic significance. In contemporary debates, the ocean economy is gaining traction with more and more littoral nations seeking to generate revenue as well as royalty from ocean resources. This paper, therefore, attempts to address the issues of the ocean economy, mineral exploration, exclusive economic zones (EEZ), interests of small island nations, and how these issues have a larger strategic implication.

Jagannath P. Panda (2014) in his work titled, *China's Tryst with the IORA: Factoring India and the Indian Ocean*[32] analyses China's overtures to the Indian Ocean Rim Association (IORA). The Indian Ocean and India are the two most immediate elements in China's policy approach to the IORA. With 20 member states, extra-territorial major powers as important dialogue partners, and the increasing importance of energy politics in the region, the IORA today is a significant multilateral body in China's calculus. Beijing's involvement with the IORA bespeaks the construct and strategy of great power. For India, China's power construct in this matter poses three challenges: Beijing as a maritime power; Beijing as an economic power; and Beijing as a polygonal power.

Suresh R. (2014) edited book on, *Maritime Security of India: The Coastal Security Challenges and Policy Options*[33] has focused on different aspects of maritime security of our country. It has covered maritime security challenges India faced in the 21st century. The book throws light on how to address such challenges so that Indian maritime interests can be fruitfully served. It has a chapter which focused on the changing perspective of maritime security after the 26/11 Mumbai terror attack incidents. It also has a chapter which addresses issues and challenges of India's maritime security. The role of the Indian navy and coast guard to meet the challenges to Indian maritime interests has also been analysed. Overall, the book can be really useful for the present study.

Gurpreet S. Khurana paper titled '*PLA Navy's Submarine Arm 'Stretches its Sea-Legs' to the Indian Ocean*[34]', featured in an edited book by Vijay Sakhuja and Gurpreet S. Khurana (2014) made a useful assessment on how China's PLA navy is making a move in the Indian Ocean. The unprecedented distant deployment of China's submarines in the Indian Ocean is a seminal development with far-reaching consequences, which may be expressed metaphorically as a traditionally 'continental' power stretching its 'sealegs'. The docking of the Chinese submarines off its southern (maritime) frontier was perceived in New Delhi as being 'unmindful to India's security concerns'. Then it argues that India would need to formulate a suitable response before its strategic options narrow down further.

In another paper by Lee Cordner (2014) titled, '*Risk Managing Maritime Security in the Indian Ocean Region*[35] analyses how maritime security in the Indian Ocean Region (IOR) has become a paramount consideration; a range of traditional and non-traditional security challenges largely converge at sea. Risk-based processes offer the potential to engage in a positive, constructive and non-confrontational approach that will help to identify collective and cooperative security strategies. Analysing the evolving maritime security risk provides a powerful tool for understanding common risks and vulnerabilities that affect regional and extra-regional actors with interests in the IOR. This can provide the impetus for diverse actors, primarily states, to cooperate to advance common objectives and protect shared interests without significantly compromising territorial integrity or sovereignty, against a range of risks that no single actor has the ability to mitigate. Maritime security cooperation in the IOR could if managed astutely and prudently, bind a diverse and largely disaggregated region.

Siraj Nizamani (2014) paper titled, *'India's Emerging Indian Ocean Strategy'*[36] focuses on understanding the emerging Indian strategic thinking on the Indian Ocean. The Indian maritime doctrine provides a guiding principle for increasing the capabilities, peace operations and rescue missions of the Indian Navy and a means for giving India a leadership role in the Indian Ocean region. The paper also covers India's maritime strength, compulsions and ambitions in the changing security environment of the 21st century. The paper argues that the Indian thrust to operate deep into the Indian Ocean enables it to go for extended military buildup and blue water capabilities. It also highlights India's maritime cooperation with other countries.

Shishir Upadhyaya (2014) paper named, *"Maritime Security Cooperation in the Indian Ocean Region: The Role of the Indian Navy'*[37] has analysed maritime cooperation strategy for India that would enable India to leverage its naval power in order to meet the challenges of the post-Cold War era. The changing maritime security scenario in the post-Cold War era is reflected in the transformation of naval doctrines, strategies and force structures evident in several Indian Ocean navies. There is an increasing focus on combating against the common non-traditional threats of the region through naval cooperation. India, as the largest naval power in the region, has a moral responsibility to foster maritime security cooperation in the region and ensure the security of shipping in the Indian Ocean. The paper argues that for India, in order to preserve a favourable balance of power in the Indian Ocean, in the face of a rising China and an adversarial Pakistan, and to maintain good order and peace amidst emerging non-traditional threats of the twenty-first century, it is imperative to maintain an all-round balanced naval capability.

Sarabjeet Singh Parmar (2014) in his well-written paper on '*Maritime Security in the Indian Ocean: An Indian Perspective*'[38] has analysed Indian long-term interests in the Indian Ocean. In doing so the paper has argued that maritime security of the Indian Ocean Region (IOR) and, specifically, its approach to maritime security has a long historical legacy. Further, the paper looks at how India's conception of maritime security in the IOR has been affected by the developments that have taken place in recent years. Taking into account the maritime challenges, India has developed a maritime strategy to ensure the security of maritime interests.

S. K. Mishra paper titled '*India's Maritime Stakes in the Indian Ocean and their Internal Spill-over Effects*'[39] in an edited book by Rajendra Prasad and Atul Chand (2014), has discussed India's maritime interests and stakes in the Indian Ocean. The security environment at sea has changed dramatically in the post-Cold War scenario. The paper argued in favour of India playing a crucial role in ensuring peace and order in the Indian Ocean. India's strategic location in the Indian Ocean puts it in a unique position to help combat maritime terror on the high seas, especially against highly valued economic targets. The paper calls upon the urgent need for the government to focus on the safety and security of the sea-lanes.

David Scott (2013) paper titled, *'India's Aspirations and Strategy for the Indian Ocean: Securing the Waves'*[40] analysed how India hopes to secure its own position against a perceived growing Chinese challenge in the Indian Ocean. The paper argues that the Indian Navy has clear-enough aspirations for the Indian Ocean which are being supported by the government. Further, it argues that various successful strategies designed to further these aspirations mean that India is gaining a sought-after position of some eminence in the Indian Ocean. It also discusses India's effort to ensure security in the Indian Ocean by adopting multiple pro-active approaches such as naval diplomacy, military exercises, etc.

Lydelle Joubert (2013) paper, *'The Extent of Maritime Terrorism and Piracy: A Comparative Analysis'*[41] makes a comparative analysis of the threats posed by maritime terrorism and piracy based on past and present experience. The attacks on the USS Cole in 2000 and on the French-registered oil tanker, Limburg, in 2002 coupled with the terrorist attacks on the United States of America (US) on 11 September 2001 (9/11), created fear that a captured ship could be used as a delivery platform for weapons of mass destruction (WMD) or that a ship with dangerous cargo could be used as a weapon. The paper argues that more attention should be paid to deviations in pirate tactics or geographical operational areas in order to detect any potential terrorist attacks to take timely preventative measures. The most dangerous situation is probably not the collaboration of pirates and terrorists, but when a terrorist attack is mistakenly identified as a piracy incident, as the consequences and preventative measures relating to these two situations will differ considerably.

Krishnappa Venkatshamy (2013) in his paper titled, *The Indian Ocean Region in India's Strategic Futures: Looking Out to 2030*[42] examines India's strategic calculus in the Indian Ocean by the year 2030. The Indian Ocean has found renewed emphasis in strategic geopolitical discourse and will play an increasing role in global security considerations in the coming decades. From the arc of Islam and Africa on its western reaches to Australia on its east, the vast expanse of the Indian Ocean Region (IOR) and its adjacent waters are considered to be the theatre of conflict and competition in the twenty-first century. The geopolitics of the IOR will have wider implications on the transformations taking place in Asia, the global economy, and key global relationships. Though geopolitical movements, amidst the rise of China and India, have set the context for viewing the importance of the IOR in a new light, the strategic imperatives of several enduring trends make the region a hotbed of global challenges.

Jonathan Holslag (2013) article titled, *The Reluctant Pretender: China's Evolving Presence in the Indian Ocean*[43], analyses China's evolving presence in the Indian Ocean. It posits that despite various traditional and non-traditional threats, the Indian Ocean is not the foremost concern in China's quest for maritime security. As a result, China's efforts to make foray beyond the Strait of Malacca remain limited. Three patterns in its posturing can be distinguished. First, it seeks to deter India – its main counterweight in South Asia – where it is the weakest, that is along the continental border. Second, it explores ways to reduce its reliance on the long maritime lifelines in the Indian Ocean. Third, it is gradually and modestly increasing its presence in a way that can be described as *diffuse pervasion*. There is thus no reason to be overly alarmed. Yet, important uncertainties remain over China's future intentions and the degree to which problems with lesser powers can prompt it to use military means to defend its interests. Future Chinese naval assertiveness in the region will more likely be the outcome of contingency than strategic provision.

Peter Lehr (2013) article titled, *Piracy and Maritime*

Governance in the Indian Ocean[44], explain why regime building is so difficult in the latter as compared to the former two, and why newly formed regimes tend to end up as 'sandbanks of shattered hope' soon after their inauguration. It conducted a comparative study on regime building in the world's three maritime 'megaregions', i.e., the Atlantic, the Asia-Pacific and the Indian Ocean. Many reasons were offered both by the author's numerous respondents and by the author himself, but amongst the findings was the widely shared opinion of specialists from various Indian Ocean Rim countries that attempts at regime building tended to fail because their aims and objectives were too lofty. Rather, it was argued that regime-building attempts should start on the relatively modest level of confidence-building measures which all potential participants could agree on, such as disaster relief, search and rescue, sustainable development of marine resources, fisheries protection, and the fight against piracy.

PK Ghosh in his work named, *'Enhancing Maritime Cooperation: The Case of India and China*[45] in an edited book by Klaus Lange et al. (2012) has explored the commonalities in maritime challenges faced by India and China. It highlights the congruence of maritime interests and suggests some response strategies to overcome the hurdles in the way of closer maritime cooperation. Indian and Chinese interests converge when it comes to ensuring maritime security by close cooperation against all sorts of maritime threats which arises from piracy and maritime terrorism. Both sides will benefit by working together to ensure the security of the sea lanes of communications. Realising the need for cooperation, India and China have in recent year's increased military-to-military cooperation which includes joint military exercises.

V.M. Mishra and Ramakant Dubey (2012) combined paper titled, *Maritime Security Challenges in South Asia and its Implications for India*[46] in an edited book by V.N. Arora et al. has analysed the various issues and challenges to maritime security in South Asia and how this will have its implications for India. The book highlighted the need for India to take the initiative of cooperating with the neighbouring countries to deal with the challenges of seaborne threats. It also focuses on the changing role of Navy and Coast Guard in meeting such challenges thereby serving Indian maritime interests.

R.S. Vasan (2012) in his well-written paper on *India's Maritime Core interests'*[47] has underlined the core maritime interests of India. The national maritime interests of India are distinctly different from the ones identified by the Indian navy and need to be analysed to understand the nuances and the dimensions of such interests so as to promote India's maritime power potential. It identifies core maritime interests and suggests a synergised approach for bringing all the stakeholders under a common umbrella to provide the necessary impetus for nation-building and to provide leverages when required. Such a process would enhance India's national status as a maritime power of eminence in this century of the seas.

Pervaiz Iqbal Cheema (2012) paper on '*Indian Ambitions in the Indian Ocean and the Pacific Rim: The Response of Global and Regional Powers'*[48] oversee the increased significance of the Indian Ocean region, followed by naval expansion by India and its ambitions. It also focuses on the interests of the key players in the Indian Ocean and then goes on to discuss the interplay of the regional and global powers. The paper argues that for India to be able to play the role of great power in the Indian Ocean, it needed not only an acknowledged dominant position in the South Asian strategic environment but also the ability to act as the local policeman. The major causes of instability in the Indian Ocean region are terrorism, piracy, illegal fishing, regional conflicts, militarization, the presence of non-state actors and weak regional organizations. While many countries of the region continue to experience terrorism, piracy is confined to certain areas such as the South China Sea, the Straits of Malacca, the Bay of Bengal and the Arabian Sea, off the Somali coast. Various areas of the Indian Ocean region continue to be plagued by regional conflicts.

David Michel and Russell Sticklor (2012) edited book on the *Indian Ocean Rising: Maritime Security and Policy Challenges*[49] explores the many policy challenges and opportunities facing the Indian Ocean. It also examines the various ways that the intertwining forces of economic growth, natural resource development, and climate change will impact coastal communities of the Indian Ocean littoral in the coming years and decades. The variety of sources of insecurity that afflict the region, ranging from insurgent conflict, terrorism, and political instability to illicit trafficking and piracy has been discussed. These security threats exist within one of the world's most important strategic and commercial spaces, with the Persian Gulf serving as the world market's most significant source of crude oil and the northern Indian Ocean rim. Among all the seaborne threats, piracy and maritime terrorism have earned the greatest share of headlines in terms of security threats in the Indian Ocean, other security issues abound.

Toshi Yoshihara (2012) in his paper titled, *Chinese Views of India in the Indian Ocean: A Geopolitical Perspective*[50] has focused on Chinese analysts steeped in the realpolitik tradition. These intellectuals and strategists discern a troubling trend towards intense competition and zero-sum interactions in the Indian Ocean. In their view, a progressively assertive India will set the pace of the impending maritime rivalries among the great powers. The article argues that if such a grim forecast takes hold in Beijing, power plays already underway in the Indian Ocean will likely become more pronounced and contentious.

Martin N. Murphy (2012) article titled, *The Abundant Sea: Prospects for Maritime Non-State Violence in the Indian Ocean*[51], oversee maritime violence perpetrated by non-state actors is a feature of the Indian Ocean. This includes the piracy, which has occurred most prominently off Somalia but also in the waters of Bangladesh, India and Indonesia, and terrorism perpetrated by al-Qaeda, the Tamil separatist movement in Sri Lanka, the Liberation Tigers of Tamil Eelam (LTTE), and the Pakistani Islamist group Lashkar-e-Taiba (LeT) against the Indian city of Mumbai. This paper aims to chart why opportunities for non-state actors to use violence to advance their interests may continue across the region.

Douglas Guilfoyle (2012) article titled, *International Law and Counter-Piracy in the Indian Ocean*[52] discusses Somali piracy in the Indian Ocean and its challenges to global trade. It is now largely conducted in the language of law enforcement, not war or terrorism. The paper explains in a brief and practical way to non-lawyers the relevant legal categories and controversies surrounding Somali piracy and to suggest why the response to piracy has remained in the law enforcement 'box'. It does this by considering piracy through the lens of four legal 'paradigms': the law of armed conflict; the international law of piracy; the law of terrorism (including terrorist financing); and the law applicable to transnational organised crime. The contention will be that the law enforcement paradigm is not only legally justifiable but also highly pragmatic and that the other categories may hold fewer benefits than observers might assume.

Dennis Rumley, T. Doyle and S. Chaturvedi (2012) joint article named, *Securing' the Indian Ocean? Competing Regional Security Constructions*[53] discusses in length regional security structure in the Indian Ocean. Dictated and driven to a significant extent by the changing dynamics of the knowledge-power equation, regional constructions are devised and propagated for a range of purposes – describing economic success, structuring a set of relationships, reproducing a particular vision of insecurity or organising a specific function, such as to maximise economic cooperation, to minimise insecurity or to fashion a particular form of security architecture. It is argued that there are three competing regional constructions for security (currently in circulation) in the Indian Ocean Region, emanating largely from Australia, the United States and India – an Indian Ocean-wide concept, an East Indian Ocean construct and an Indo-Pacific concept. It is suggested that there exists an overriding narrative in favour of an 'Indo-Pacific' construction at the expense of Indian Ocean concepts. As a result, it is concluded that the Indian Ocean Rim Association for Regional Cooperation (IOR-ARC) will remain relatively weak for the foreseeable future and that, unless there is a concerted attempt to involve China in a new maritime security regime, the discourse and practices of regional security might become the preserve of an Indo-Pacific alliance comprising Australia, India, the United States and other East Asian states, including Japan.

Chunhao Lou (2012), *US–India–China Relations in the Indian Ocean: A Chinese Perspective*[54] explores the growing interests and competition for countries such as the United States, China and India. The Indian Ocean Region (IOR) is becoming increasingly significant in the world arena, with the United States, India and China—the most important stakeholders in the region—playing substantial roles. Since the three countries face similar security challenges and share common interests in the IOR, it is necessary for them to compete to a reasonable extent while pushing forward with functional cooperation. Because of the existence of an interdependent relationship and common security challenges, the future scenario will be one of dynamic and manageable competition, instead of inevitable conflict and rivalry.

R.S. Vasan (2011) in his paper titled, *"Maritime Piracy: Challenges and the Way Ahead"*[55], has analysed the challenges of piracy to Indian maritime security in the 21st century. The paper argues that there is a need for coordinated effort on two other fronts as part of a comprehensive multilateral strategy, viz. legal, as in the development of judicial institutions and procedural recourse/remedies for accused pirates; and socio-economic, as in help for former fishermen, now pirates, to return to livelihoods that may be low yield but are also low risk. The paper attracted the attention of one serious dimension of the pirate-terrorist nexus which has emerged in recent years. As against the rising security concerns of the maritime threats particularly, the paper has highlight ways and means on how to respond to such challenges.

Swaran Singh (2011) article titled, *China's Forays into the Indian Ocean: Strategic Implications for India*[56] analyses China's expanding influence in the Indian Ocean. So far it has been sporadic, seasonal, and restricted. Often, these are triggered by and remain limited to reporting new assets and technologies in China's naval modernisation and fail to appreciate their larger vision, deeper stimuli and also their complex linkages to China's political compulsions, economic motives and social moorings. The naval component of China's Indian Ocean policy, therefore, needs to be put in perspective and these analyses need to explore China's forays into the Indian Ocean in terms of its larger and concerted initiatives in building a maritime infrastructure both across the Indian Ocean littoral and also in expanding its ocean-faring and ocean-exploring claims and capabilities. What is also necessary to appreciate is how, in the face of new threats of maritime terrorism and the expanding US presence on China's periphery, China feels not only isolated but even targeted. All of this makes China far more assertive in accessing the Indian Ocean with obvious implications for its neighbours especially peer-powers like India that share several of China's proclivities. India, however, must carefully sidestep from falling prey to popular binaries of friend-or-foe formulations and focus not just on narrower and surface-level trends in China's naval build-up, but expand its appreciation and engage China across the whole spectrum of maritime sectors and thereby maximise mutual benefits and lasting stable maritime equations with China.

Donald Berlin (2011) article titled, *The Rise of India and the Indian Ocean*[57] analyses how India seeks to potentially achieve the regional influence in the Indian Ocean to which it aspires. To this end, New Delhi has raised its profile and strengthened its position in a variety of states on the Indian Ocean littoral, especially Iran, Sri Lanka, Burma, Singapore, Thailand and most of the Ocean's small island states. India has also become a more palpable presence in some of the Ocean's key maritime zones, particularly the Bay of Bengal and the Andaman Sea. Of equal or greater importance, India's links with the most important external actors in the Indian Ocean – the United States, Japan, Israel and France – have also been upgraded. These are significant achievements and derive both from India's growing economic clout and the surer hand of contemporary Indian diplomacy. Gaps, of course, remain in India's strategic posture. The paper argues that New Delhi will need to strengthen further its hand in coastal Africa and the Arabian Peninsula. More work will also be required to upgrade India's still somewhat distant relationship with Australia. At the same time, India will need to be more skilful than it has been in cultivating – or 'compelling' – better relations and an environment more attuned to its interests in Pakistan and Bangladesh. As India pursues its various goals in the Indian Ocean, much will depend on the performance of the Indian economy and on India's ability to avoid domestic communal discord. Another variable will be the extent to which other states – particularly China and the United States, but also Pakistan and others in southern Asia – are willing or able to offer serious resistance to India's ambitions. This development will have a transforming effect on the Indian Ocean basin and eventually the world.

Arun Prakash has contributed a paper titled *'The Rationale and Implications of India's Growing Maritime Power'*[58] in an edited book by Michael Kugleman (2011) in which he has highlighted the key rationale behind India's maritime power. He asserts that India's maritime growth can help strengthen its strategic position vis-à-vis Pakistan. This is because greater Indian sea-based power projection will compensate for what Prakash describes as India's "serious asymmetry." India has declared a no-first-use nuclear policy, he explains, while Pakistan has maintained a "deliberately am-biguous" threat of unilateral first-use that enables it to escalate small battles into nuclear conflict whenever it wishes. However, by staging robust maritime manoeuvre activities to support the Indian Army, India could deter Pakistani "adventurism" without approaching Pakistan's "unknown nuclear threshold."

Hari Saran and Harsh K. Sinha (2011) paper titled, *'India's Maritime Stakes and Challenges in the Indian Ocean*[59], evaluate India's maritime developments and interests in the 21st century in general and analyses regional challenges in particular. The paper argued that without developing adequate maritime strategy and power one cannot attain the desired status in the global hierarchy. India is a conventional and maritime power. India's regional maritime identity has undergone a major change during the past two decades. India now has become a regional maritime power. It also discusses maritime threats to India's security such as Piracy/ Hijacking, trafficking of Small Arms and Drugs, Maritime Terrorism, Illegal Migration/ Human smuggling, etc.

Lee Cordner (2010) paper titled, *Maritime Security in the Indian Ocean Region: Compelling and Convergent Agendas'*[60] examines the way in which Indian Ocean region (IOR) is fast becoming a major area of global political and security interest. The region's political and security context is quickly changing due to expanding and competing for Chinese and Indian spheres of influence along with relatively declining United States power. The study argues that greater attention needs to be given to Indian Ocean maritime security and the development of IOR maritime security regimes need to be pursued as a matter of urgency. Further, it spelt out the traditional security concerns like maintenance of the freedom of maritime navigation and unfettered access to and transport of vital energy supplies are increasing in importance in the Indian Ocean. In addition, non-traditional security threats emanating from the impacts of climate change and the effects of population and industrial growth are presenting major resource management and environmental, human and food security challenges. These security challenges largely converge in the maritime domain. It is imperative that IOR-wide maritime security cooperation be progressed. Regional and extra-regional nation-states have interests to protect and capacities to contribute to IOR security.

Christian Bouchard and William Crumplin (2010) joint article titled *'Neglected No Longer: The Indian Ocean At The Forefront of World Geopolitics and Global Geostrategy*[61] analyses how the Indian Ocean and its bordering states have been of growing significance in world geopolitics and global geostrategy. It views the Indian Ocean region of great diversity and contrasts in terms of politics, population, economy and environment, as well as being a complex geopolitical framework where foreign powers and local states' interests deeply intermingle. Since the end of the Cold War, the region has been in a period of great instability and regional rearrangement that is still ongoing today. Taking into account the significance of its strategic energy resources, the importance of its strategic shipping lanes, the 'rise of India' as a dominant regional player, the turbulences of the Islamic world, the deep and broad involvement of the United States (and its allies) in the region, as well as China's recent entry on the regional chessboard. The paper argues that there is no doubt that the Indian Ocean will remain at the forefront of world geopolitics in the coming decades and most probably for the entire twenty-first century.

David Brewster (2010) in his work titled, *"An Indian Sphere of Influence in the Indian Ocean*[62]*"*, has examined India's maritime ambitions and relationships in the Indian Ocean and ask whether this may presage an extended Indian sphere of influence in the region. India's strategic ambitions in the Indian Ocean have been highlighted. It also gives an overview of the growth of maritime perspectives in Indian strategic thinking and the expansion of India's naval capabilities. The paper argued that India's increased enthusiasm for maritime power has been accompanied by an expansion in India's naval capabilities. India has over the last decade or so been quietly expanding its influence throughout the Indian Ocean. The Indian Navy has been active in developing security relationships that are intended to enhance India's ability to project power and restrict China's ability to develop security relationships in the region.

Robert D. Kaplan (2010) has in one of his well-written volume titled *'Monsoon: The Indian Ocean and the Future of American* Power'[63] analyses China's rise as a great power and its interests in the Indian Ocean region. He is of the view that China seeks to ensuring and securing its vital energy supplies. He further made an argument that the Indian Ocean is the arena where Sino-US and Sino-Indian rivalries may potentially flash out in the future due to the need for securing their respective national interests with respect to national security, energy security and the like.

While C. Uday Bhaskar (2010) article titled, *China and India in the Indian Ocean Region: Neither Conflict nor Cooperation Preordained'*[64] the competition between the two Asian rivals in the Indian Ocean. China and India have divergent political ideologies, characteristics, aspirations, anxieties and hence their strategic perceptions and orientations differ. To serve its long-term national interests in the Indian Ocean, PLA Navy (PLAN) now deploys almost 260 naval vessels which are far ahead of India which deploys just under 100 naval vessels.

P. V. Rao (2010) essay on '*Indian Ocean Maritime Security Cooperation: The Employment of Navies and Other Maritime Forces*'[65] discusses how after the collapse of the Cold War system, there emerged major threats from non-state actors. This has fundamentally transformed the maritime security environment in the Indian Ocean Region (IOR). Consequently, navies in the region are redefining their roles and responsibilities to combat the new threats to maritime security. Naval forces in the region are under pressure to modernise and to upgrade their capabilities to meet contemporary challenges. The division between high sea and constabulary roles is narrowing. Regional and extra-regional powers in the IOR have recognised the imperative of promoting cooperation between respective maritime forces to combat the new threats. A variety of naval forces such as naval warships, coast guards, marine police and commandos are being employed to ensure 'good order at sea'.

Kunwar Rejendra Singh (2008) in his book titled, *Maritime Security for India: New Challenges and Responses*[66], evaluates India's maritime defence capability in the face of the emerging maritime challenges. It also analyses different dimension of maritime challenges that are most likely to be posed as also options that are available to neutralise them. The book argues that the Indian elite has over the last few decades taken slow but steady steps in the field of maritime development. It also explores India's maritime security cooperation with regional and global powers. The author in this book has called upon the need for strengthening Indian maritime security forces including navy and coast guard to deal with all sorts of maritime threats vis-a-vis maritime terrorism, piracy, etc. In response to changing maritime environment, India has in recent times geared up maritime security capability under several inter-related heads such as sub-surface warfare, naval-air armament, surface combatants, amphibious warfare, force projection capability, etc.

Sam Bateman (2006) in his paper, '*Assessing the Threat*

of Maritime Terrorism: Issues for the Asia-Pacific Region'[67] makes a critical assessment of the contemporary threat of maritime terrorism in the Asia-Pacific region. It addresses the operational dimensions of the threat to ships and port infrastructure and considers the effectiveness of the international and regional measures that have been introduced in recent years to deal with this threat. Based on a proposition that there has been rather too much emphasis on highly remote and speculative "doomsday" scenarios, the article supports the need for balance and equity in addressing the risks of maritime terrorism. It identifies types of terrorist attacks that might be assessed as more credible, as well as some that might be considered less credible.

D. Walgreen (2006) in his paper titled, *China in the Indian Ocean Region: Lessons in PRC Grand Strategy'*[68] underlines China's growing influence in the Indian Ocean region. The paper argues that Checking India's rising powers in the Indian Ocean Region is a critical juncture for Beijing. To this end, China exerts a strategy to maintain good relations with the IOR littoral states. Sharing the same cynicism toward India, Pakistan is a valuable surrogate to provide counter-weight to India in the region'. China is engaged in dirty games of providing the arms and equipment needs to Indian neighbours.

Donald L. Berlin (2006) in his paper titled, *"India in the Indian Ocean"*[69] has focused primarily on issues in the IOR. He does not spell out the Indian maritime strategy instead he does provide an overview of Indian interests in the Indian Ocean by examining its relations with key powers and some of the elements of Indian maritime capability to support its strategy. His examination is an outside-in perspective, which relates what responses should be taken by others as a result of Indian developments; whereas I am looking to underscore the Indian response to its internal and external realities and developments.

Admiral Arun Prakash (2005), former Indian Navy's Chief of Naval Staff, in his notable work on the paper entitled, *"Future Strategy and Challenges for the Indian Navy"*[70] has briefly mentioned India's objectives and naval capabilities, but does not really provide any depth to the argument. This article spurred my interest in the subject and underscores the importance of providing more depth and clarity in order to better understand the Indian rationale for its decisions.

Anand Mathur (2002) has in his work titled, *'Growing Importance of the Indian Ocean in the Post-Cold War Era and its Implications for India*[79] explains the growing significance of Indian Ocean from the Indian point of view. It dwells on the connection between the Indian Ocean and India's Security in the changing world's security scenario. It highlights India's maritime interests in the Indian Ocean in the aftermath of the Cold War. With the beginning of Operation 'Enduring Freedom', the Indian Ocean region became all the more important in the free market world as the new silk route passes through it. The discovery of oil and natural gas in the Caspian Sea induced intense competition, making this region a dangerous potential flashpoint of global significance. The Indian Ocean has been of distinct strategic, economic and ecological value for India. Peninsular India needs to exploit its oceanic opportunities to emerge as a nation whose global relevance is commensurate with its size.

Vijay Sakhuja (2001) in his paper titled, 'The *Indian Ocean and the Safety of Sea Lanes of Communication*[80] analyses the geo-strategic and geo-economic significance of the security of sea lanes of communication in the Indian Ocean. Sea lines of communication comprise the umbilical cord of a state's economy and the arteries of a region's economic health. During times of peace, they serve as commercial trade routes but during the war, these routes are considered strategic pathways to keep the war machine fully oiled. Today, these routes are being threatened by piracy, drug trafficking, gun-running, human smuggling, pollution, accidents, inter state conflicts and territorial disputes. None is independent of the other and failure in one often leads to failure in others. This calls for greater cooperation among states to enhance security and safety of maritime enterprise.

Rahul Roy Chaudhury (1995) has written a very good book on *India's Maritime Security*[81] which highlight the importance of effectively dealing with the compulsions and complexities of India's maritime security necessitates a sophisticated, and often, complicated, the interplay of the country's economic, foreign and defence policies. The book has thoroughly analysed the maritime policy of our country in the context of the emerging threats to our maritime security and interests. In another well-written book by Rahul Roy-Chaudhury (1995) titled *Sea Power and Indian Security* [55] underscored the value of sea power for India. The study gave a detailed overview of the growth and expansion of the Indian navy up to the late 1980s, in response to India's perceived threats. It also examines the cause/effect relationship between India and its adversaries which will undoubtedly continue to have utility in the current period. Unfortunately, a threat-based analysis only explains a portion of India's maritime history. This thesis contends that its current strategy accounts for not just the threat element, but also the element of interests and capabilities.

The first work on the subject was being reviewed is by K. M. Panikkar, a renowned historian with significant diplomatic experience in the post-independence period which examines India's strategic picture in that period with a view toward the need for developing greater defense capabilities than economic development and growth. Panikkar's notable work on the subject is contained in his 1945 book on *India and the Indian Ocean*[82] which analysed the influence of sea power in the Indian context, and his 1960 book titled *Problems of Indian Defense*[83] which dedicates a chapter to naval strategy. He provides a sound and rational argument for expanding India's naval forces, especially given the strategic picture of that time. While his work was the foundational piece which indicated India's quest to develop its naval force during the post-independence period, India's recent ascendancy in economic and political terms has made his work largely irrelevant in today's world.

References

1. G S Khurana, "Maritime Security in the Indian Ocean: Convergence Plus Cooperation Equals Resonance", Strategic Analysis, Vol. 28, No. 3, July-September 2004, p. 413.
2. Mohan Malik, China and India: Great Power Rivals (Lynne Reiner Publishers, 2011), p. 325.
3. K. M. Panikkar, India and the Indian Ocean: An Essay on the Influence of Sea Power on Indian History (London: George Allen and Unwin, 1945), pp. 84-5.
4. Quoted in Rahul Roy-Chaudhury, Sea Power and Indian Security (London: Brassey's, 1995), p. 199.
5. H. J. Mackinder, Democratic Ideals and Reality (London: Constable & Co., 1919).
6. See, Cowles Encyclopedia of Nations (New York: Cowles Education Corporation, 1968), p. 246.
7. Ajey Lele, "India and the Indian Ocean Region: An Appraisal", Claws Journal, Winter 2008, p. 171. Also refer to W. Lawrence S. Prabhakar, "Growth of Naval Power in the Indian Ocean: Dynamics and Transformation", National Maritime Foundation Monograph Series, New Delhi, 2016, pp. 8-9
8. Robert D. Kaplan, "Center Stage for the 21st Century: Power Plays in the Indian Ocean", Foreign Affairs, March/April 2009, pp. 16-18.
9. Ajey Lele, n. 7, pp. 172-73.
10. R. D. Kaplan, n. 8, p. 19.
11. Sardar FS Lodhi, "The Indian Ocean and Our Security", available at <http://www.sagecenter.org/en/node/9>.

12. Maleehah Iman Ali, "The implications of China's 'String of Pearls Strategy' on Relations with Indian Ocean Nations", Under Graduate Dissertation, Lingnan University, Hong Kong, 2013, available at <*http://commons.ln.edu.hk/socsci_fyp/3*>.
13. Thean Potgieter, "Maritime Security in the Indian Ocean: Strategic Setting and Features", Institute for Security Studies, No. 236, August 2012, p. 2
14. K. M. Panikkar, n. 3, p. 19.
15. Peter Lehr, "The Challenge of Security in the Indian Ocean in the 21st Century: Plus ca Change", Working Paper, No. 13, South Asia Institute, Department of Political Science, University of Heidelberg, November 2002, p.
16. 3 Senator Claiborne Pell, Challenge of the Seven Seas (New York: William Morrow & Co. Inc., 1966), p. 27.
17. D. Rumley, et al. (eds.), The Security of Sea Lanes of Communication in the Indian Ocean Region (Kaula Lampur: Maritime Institute of Malaysia, 2007).
18. Refer to this site, <*http://geography.knoji.com/facts-about-the-indian-ocean/*>.
19. R.C. Sharma, Oceanography for Geography (Allahabad, 1970), p. 83.
20. Ibid, p. 57.
21. Lee Cordner, "Proceedings from the Indian Ocean Maritime Security Symposium", Australia Defence College, 15-17 April 2009, p. 9.
22. Raja Javed Afzal, "A Regional Perspective on Indian Ocean Maritime Security Issues", in the '*Proceedings from the Indian Ocean Maritime Security Symposium*', Australia Defence College, 15-17 April 2009, p. 40.
23. See, 'Indian Ocean Region and its Geo-politics, Indian Maritime Strategy', available at <*http://www.indiannavy.gov.in*>
24. See, World Oil Transit Choke Points, Country Analysis Briefs, Energy Information Administration (EIA). January 2008.

25. Ibid.
26. Andreea, "The Strait of Malacca: The Meeting Point of Giants", The World Reporter, 4 May 2012, available at <*http://www.theworldreporter.com/2012/05/strait-of-malacca-meeting-point-of.html*>.
27. Andrew S. Erickson, et al., "Diego Garcia and the United States- Emerging Indian Ocean Strategy", Asian Survey, Vol. 6, No. 3 (2010), p. 216.
28. Walter C. Ladwing, "Delhi's Pacific Ambition: Naval Power, Look East, and India's Emerging Influence in the Asia-Pacific", Asian Survey, Vol. 5, No. 2, 2009, pp. 87-92.
29. Integrated Headquarters (Navy), Indian Maritime Doctrine, 2009, p. 58.
30. David Michel, et al., "Natural Resources in the Indian Ocean: Fisheries and Minerals", in David Michel and Russell Sticklor (eds.), Indian Ocean Rising: Maritime Security and Policy Challenges (Washington: Stimson, July 2012), p. 103.
31. Robert Kaplan, n. 8, p. 16.
32. Rupert Herbert-Burns, "Energy in the Indian Ocean Region: Vital Features and New Frontiers", in David Michel and Russell Sticklor (eds.), Indian Ocean Rising: Maritime Security and Policy Challenges (Washington: Stimson, July 2012), p. 89.
33. Manickam Venkataraman, "Piracy off the Coast of Somalia: Implications for China's Maritime Security", Bandung Journal of Global South, Vol. 3, No. 5, 2016.
34. Sam Bateman, "Maritime Security Governance in the Indian Ocean Region", Journal of Indian Ocean Region, Vol. 12, No. 1, 2016.
35. Sharifah M. Alatas, "India's Maritime Strategy in the Indian Ocean Region: Issues of Strategic Culture", Journal of South Asian Studies, Vol. 3, No. 3, 2015.
36. Eryan Ramadhani, "China in the Indian Ocean Region: The Confined 'Far-Seas Operation", India Quarterly-The Journal of International Affairs, Vol. 71, No. 2, June 2015.

37. P.K. Ghosh, "Evolving Indian Ocean Governance Architecture: An Indian Perspective", Journal of the Indian Ocean Region, Vol. 11, No. 2, 2015.
38. Pankaj K. Jha, "Mineral Explorations in the Indian Ocean: India's Policy Response", Maritime Affairs: Journal of the National Maritime Foundation of India, Vol. 11, No. 1, 2015.
39. Jagannath P. Panda, "China's Tryst with the IORA: Factoring India and the Indian Ocean", Strategic Analysis, Vol. 38, No. 5, September 2014.
40. Suresh R. (ed.), Maritime Security of India: The Coastal Security Challenges and Policy Options (New Delhi: Vij Books India Pvt. Ltd., 2014).
41. Vijay Sakhuja and Gurpreet S. Khurana (eds.), Maritime Perspective 2014 (New Delhi: National Maritime Foundation, 2015).
42. Lee Cordner, "Risk Managing Maritime Security in the Indian Ocean Region", Journal of Indian Ocean Region, Vol. 10, No. 1, June 2014.
43 Siraj Nizamani, "India's Emerging Indian Ocean Strategy", IPRI Journal, Vol. XIV, No. 1, Winter 2014.
44. Shishir Upadhyaya, "Maritime security cooperation in the Indian Ocean Region: The role of the Indian Navy", Australian Journal of Maritime and Ocean Affairs, Vol. 6, No. 4, June 2014.
45. Sarabjeet Singh Parmar, "Maritime Security in the Indian Ocean: An Indian Perspective", Journal of Defence Studies, Vol. 8, No. 1, January-March 2014.
46. Rajendra Prasad and Atul Chand (eds.), India's Internal Security Challenges (New Delhi: Mohit Publications, 2014).
47. David Scott, "India's Aspirations and Strategy for the Indian Ocean: Securing the Waves", The Journal of Strategic Studies, Vol. 36, No. 4, 2013.
48. Lydelle Joubert, "The Extent of Maritime Terrorism and Piracy: A Comparative Analysis", Scientia Militaria, South African Journal of Military Studies, Vol. 41, No. 1, 2013

49. Krishnappa Venkatshamy, "The Indian Ocean Region in India's Strategic Futures: Looking Out to 2030", Journal of the Indian Ocean Region, Vol. 9, No. 1, June 2013.
50. Jonathan Holslag, "The Reluctant Pretender: China's Evolving Presence in The Indian Ocean", Journal of Indian Ocean Region, Vol. 9, No. 1, June 2013.
51. Peter Lehr, "Piracy and Maritime Governance in the Indian Ocean", Journal of Indian Ocean Region, Vol. 9, No. 1, June 2013.
52. Klaus Lange, et al., (eds.), *Revisiting Contemporary South Asia: Politics, Economics & Security* (New Delhi: Pentagon Press, 2012).
53. V. N. Arora, et al, New Dimensions of Security Challenges in South Asia: Diagnosis and Prognosis (New Delhi: Mohit Publications, 2012).
54. R.S. Vasan, "India's Maritime Core Interests", Strategic Analysis, Vol. 36, No. 3, May 2012.
55. Pervaiz Iqbal Cheema, "Indian Ambitions in the Indian Ocean and the Pacific Rim: The Response of Global and Regional Powers", Journal of European Studies, Vol. 28, No. 2, July 2012.
56. David Michel and Russell Sticklor (eds.), Indian Ocean Rising: Maritime Security and Policy Challenges (Washington: Stimson, July 2012).
57. Toshi Yoshihara, "Chinese Views of India in the Indian Ocean: A Geopolitical Perspective", Strategic Analysis, Vol. 36, No. 3, May 2012.
58. Martin N. Murphy, "The Abundant Sea: Prospects for Maritime Non-State Violence in the Indian Ocean", Journal of Indian Ocean Region, Vol. 8, No. 2, December 2012.
59. Douglas Guilfoyle, "International Law and Counter-Piracy in the Indian Ocean", Journal of Indian Ocean Region, Vol. 8, No. 2, December 2012.
60. Dennis Rumley, T. Doyle and S. Chaturvedi, "Securing' the Indian Ocean? Competing Regional Security Constructions', Journal of the Indian Ocean Region, Vol. 8, No. 2, June 2012.

61. Chunhao Lou, "US–India–China Relations in the Indian Ocean: A Chinese Perspective", Strategic Analysis, Vol. 36, No. 4, July-August 2012.
62. R.S. Vasan, "Maritime Piracy: Challenges and the Way Ahead", Jindal Journal of International Affairs, Vol. 1, No. 1, October 2011.
63. Swaran Singh, "China's Forays into the Indian Ocean: Strategic Implications for India", Journal of Indian Ocean Region, Vol. 7, No. 2, December 2011.
64. Donald Berlin, "The Rise of India and the Indian Ocean", Journal of Indian Ocean Region, Vol. 7, No. 1, June 2011.
65. Michael Kugleman (ed.), India's Contemporary Security Challenges (Washington, D.C.:Woodrow Wilson International Center for Scholars, 2011).
66. Hari Saran and Harsh K. Sinha, "India's Maritime Stakes and Challenges in Indian Ocean", Scholar's Voice: A New Way of Thinking Centre for Defence Sciences, Vol. 2, No. 1, January-June 2011.
67. Lee Cordner "Maritime Security in the Indian Ocean Region: Compelling and Convergent Agendas", Australian Journal of Maritime and Ocean Affairs, Vol. 2, No. 1, 2010.
68. Christian Bouchard and William Crumplin, "Neglected No Longer: The Indian Ocean At The Forefront of World Geopolitics and Global Geostrategy", Journal of Indian Ocean Region, Vol. 6, No. 1, June 2010.
69. David Brewster, "An Indian Sphere of Influence in Indian Ocean", Security Challenges,Vol. 6, No. 3, Spring 2010.
70. Robert D. Kaplan, Monsoon: The Indian Ocean and the Future of American Power (New York: Random House, 2010).
71. C. Uday Bhaskar, "China and India in the Indian Ocean Region: Neither Conflict nor Cooperation Preordained", China Report, Vol. 46, No, 3, August 2010.
72. P. V. Rao, "Indian Ocean Maritime Security Cooperation: The Employment of Navies and Other Maritime Forces", Journal of Indian Ocean Region, Vol. 6, No. 1, June 2010.

73. Kunwar Rejendra Singh, Maritime Security for India: New Challenges and Responses (New Delhi: New Century Publications, 2008).

74. Sam Bateman, "Assessing the Threat of Maritime Terrorism: Issues for the Asia-Pacific Region", Security Challenges, Vol. 2, No. 3, October 2006.

75. D. Walgreen, "China in the Indian Ocean Region: Lessons in PRC Grand Strategy", Comparative Strategy, Vol. 25, No. 1, 2006.

76. Donald L. Berlin, "India in the Indian Ocean", Naval War College Review, Vol. 59, No. 2, Spring 2006.

77. Arun Prakash, "Future Strategy and Challenges for the Indian Navy" in the Royal United Services Institute for Defence and Security Studies Defence Systems, Vol. 8, No.2, November 2005.

78. Anand Mathur, "Growing Importance of the Indian Ocean in the Post-Cold War Era and its Implications for India", Strategic Analysis, Vol. 26, No. 4, Oct-Dec, 2002.

79. Vijay Sakhuja, "Indian Ocean and the Safety of Sea Lanes of Communication", Strategic Analysis, Vol. XXV, No. 5, 2001.

80. Rahul Roy Chaudhury, India's Maritime Security (New Delhi: Knowledge World, June 2000).

81. Rahul Roy-Chaudhury, Sea Power and Indian Security (London: Brasseys, 1995).

82. K. M. Panikkar, India and the Indian Ocean: An Essay on the Influence of Sea Power on Indian History (London: George Allen and Unwin Ltd, 1945).

83. K. M. Panikkar, Problems of Indian Defense (London: Asia Publishing House, 1960).

2

India's Maritime Threats

India's ancient maritime tradition pre-dates Greek, Roman and Carthaginian exploits in the Mediterranean, not enough is known about it, because we had neither a Herodotus nor Thucydides to record history; and our past suffers from a lack of documentation. For this reason, we have had to accept accounts, authored by Western historians, which rarely make mention of the seafaring skills of the ancient Arabs, the Chinese, or Indians. And yet, tangible evidence of India's widespread cultural, religious and linguistic imprint – dating back 2-3 millennia - is available. It is found, not just around the Indian Ocean rim, but extending, from the Mediterranean to the Pacific.

A lone Indian voice in this historiographic void is that of Sardar KM Panikkar; statesman, diplomat and visionary. According to Panikkar, due to its earlier civilization and its predictable system of monsoon winds, it was the Indian Ocean region, and not the Mediterranean or Aegean Seas, which saw the world's first oceanic sailing activity. Arguing that ancient Hindus possessed the skills to construct sturdy ocean-going ships and knew the use of a magnetic compass for accurate navigation, he clinches his extensive arguments by stating that: *"Millenniums before Columbus sailed the Atlantic and Magellan crossed the Pacific, the Indian Ocean had become a thoroughfare of commercial and cultural traffic."*[1]

He paints a fascinating picture of India's maritime past as he describes the activities that took place in the 4th century BCE Mauryan Empire. He provides evidence that the waters of the Bay of Bengal witnessed a continuum of commercial colonization as well as cultural and religious osmosis by sea from India's east coast ports to south-east Asia. The existence of ancient Hindu kingdoms right across SE Asia, then known as *Suvarnabhumi,* is still vividly evident in the architecture, culture and religious beliefs of this region. He also reminds us that this cultural empire could not have been sustained without the endeavours of skillful and courageous Indian seafarers who braved the turbulent Bay of Bengal for generations. Significantly, Panikkar debunks the thesis that overseas travel for Hindus had been banned by a Brahmanical fiat; saying that the 'ban' perhaps applied only to people in north India.

From the 5th century AD command of the eastern waters and Malacca Straits passed into the hands of a great Indian maritime power, known as the Sri Vijaya Empire, based in Sumatra. The Sri Vijaya kings retained mastery over the surrounding waters through a powerful navy, and controlled all shipping traffic. In the year 1007 AD, the Indian Emperor Rajendra of the south Indian Chola dynasty fitted out a powerful fleet and challenged the Sri Vijayas. The ensuing 100-year war weakened both empires and heralded the serious decline of Hindu sea power.

During the 12th and 13th centuries, as Central Asian hordes poured down our mountain passes to conquer the rich Gangetic plain, India's maritime power gradually withered, and oceanic trade passed into the hands of the Arabs. In May 1498, when the Portuguese adventurer Vasco da Gama arrived off Calicut, the Sultanate of Delhi was ruled by the Afghan Lodhi Dynasty, while Southern India was divided between the Bahamini and Vijayanagaram kingdoms. None of them were blessed with a maritime vision, much less a navy; and India's maritime prowess went into rapid decline.

Fifteenth century Europe had seen many advances in the areas of shipbuilding and ocean navigation as well as metallurgy and cannon founding. We must note that it was this technological edge, which enabled European merchant-adventurers, to undertake long-distance voyages into uncharted oceans, and to overwhelm natives of eastern lands. The toe-holds they gained, in the form of trading posts, eventually metamorphosed into full blown empires.

Panikkar consistently emphasizes that India's fate has been determined not on land frontiers, but on the oceanic expanse that washes its three sides. He declares that India will be in peril if the Indian Ocean ever ceases to be a 'protected sea.' Lamenting our inherited sea-blindness, Panikkar sounded a clear warning in 1945: *"While to other countries, the Indian Ocean is only one of the oceanic areas, to India it is the vital sea. Her future is dependent on the freedom of its waters."*[2]

Threats and Challenges

There are currently two main sources of insecurity in the Indian Ocean. The first is *instability in some of the littoral and hinterland states* around the Indian Ocean.[3] This also relates to sea-based terrorist activities and maritime piracy. With regard to terrorism, prominent incidents include attacks by al-Qaeda on a US warship in 2000, and on a French tanker in 2002.[4] In the field of maritime piracy, much attention has been drawn by piracy in the Malacca Straits (especially up to 2005) and Somali piracy in the Gulf of Aden and the Western Indian Ocean (since 2008 in particular).[5] To a certain degree, both sea-based terrorism and maritime piracy threaten the security of international shipping in the Indian Ocean. Moreover, sea-based terrorism can also be aimed against targets on land. The '26/11' Mumbai attacks in 2008 are a dramatic illustration of this.

Littoral is an area where sea meets land. These spaces are rich in diversified marine living resources and are hubs of urbanization: nearly 60% of the world's population lives within 100km of the waterfront. A large number of cities with populations exceeding one million are located in coastal areas. The littorals are hubs of intense economic activity linked with maritime trade, which pivot on an intricate maritime infrastructure (ports, harbours, oil and gas terminals and rail/road system) as well as networks connecting the littoral with the hinterland. Such infrastructure provides the sinews for the economic growth and comprehensive development of the state.

Littorals provide the muscle for economic growth and development, but in some cases they can also be focal points of social dysfunction due to economic disparities. Lack of governance and an ineffective social security apparatus have in some coastal areas created favourable conditions for illegal activities.[6] In the absence of good governance, criminal and subversive elements flourish and these can disrupt social harmony. Governance of littorals is thus a major challenge for civil security agencies. Ineffective governance has also left the marine resources that littorals provide vulnerable to attack by unsustainable fishing, poaching and dumping of chemicals. These activities can generate tensions among states, and can even result in local populations taking up arms in an effort to protect their legitimate interests, as is the case in Somalia.

In essence, while littorals provide economic muscle, they are often areas of social disorder. The nexus between organized crime networks and terrorist groups with transnational capability can potentially exploit these spaces to conduct their operations, and this poses significant challenges for states.

Sea piracy has existed since ancient times and its scourge

has been well documented. The Romans and the Greeks in the Mediterranean and the Srivijaya rulers in South-East Asia dispatched navies to fight pirates and protect trade. In more recent times, stories of sea piracy have generally been restricted to romanticism on the silver screen: audiences were exposed to glamorous swashbuckling pirate and buccaneer icons such as Blackbeard, Long John Silver, Anne Bonny and Black Sam Bellamy. However, over the last 20 years the menace of piracy has had a very real impact on international shipping, with horrifying incidents of hostage-taking and assault, of crew members traumatized, left adrift or even killed. The maritime community has consistently voiced its concern about the menace of piracy and called on states to bring order at sea for the safety of crews and the security of trade.

Piracy has become the bane of the modern seafarer. The numerous cases of reported and unreported piracy have led to considerable concern and multinational efforts to control this violent menace. According to the International Maritime Organization Annual Report 2002,[7] the Malacca Straits, South China Sea and Indian Ocean are the areas that have been most affected by piracy.

This heavy infestation of piracy has a lot to do with the geography of the area, but economic conditions and the mindset of the coastal people in the hundreds of minor islands that lace the Malacca Straits and South China Sea are also a significant factor. Recently, piracy- related incidents seem to have spilled over from these two areas into the Bay of Bengal and the Arabian Sea. Indeed, the center of gravity of piracy may shift to the waters around India.

There also seems to be a distinct change in the type of piracy that is occurring. Earlier acts were of the type termed 'Asian Piracy' that often involved mere stealing of valuables from ships with a negligible amount of associated violence. However, recent cases in the region have displayed a dramatic increase in brazen violence, and the methodology has made them akin to the South American or West African type of piracy.

In addition, the involvement of organised crime in hijacking ships was evident from the 1999 *MV Alonda Rainbow* case. This case is also a modern example of various enforcement agencies acting together to fight piracy.[8] Unless law enforcement agencies of various states cooperate to bring piracy under control, this phenomenon will not only increase dramatically but may spin out of control. The portents of this problem lie in the fact that Asian operatives have become exceptionally well organized, with entrenched gangs and, at times, under state sponsorship. Their links with other forms of "maritime disorder and terrorism," such as narco–terrorism and human smuggling, are well-established and organic extensions of one another.

Maritime security has assumed a new dimension in the post 9-11 era. The fight against this old and persistent issue has received a boost with the backing of the international community, particularly the United States. While the search for terrorists and their personification in Al Qaeda continues on land, at sea the international community is hunting for Bin Laden's terror ships, termed the "phantom fleet." The main idea is to prevent Osama Bin Laden and Al Qaeda operatives from escaping via the sea or terrorizing the maritime arena.[9]

The importance of container security to maritime terrorism is only now being realized after a U.S. Navy search of a freighter in January 2002 led to the discovery of a group of Al Qaeda terrorists hiding inside a well equipped shipping container. The group escaped from the container shortly before the search commenced. This discovery prompted an increase in surveillance of ships as well as trucks carrying shipping containers leaving Afghanistan for Pakistani ports.[10] In another case, a suspected Al Qaeda terrorist smuggled himself halfway around the world inside a shipping container that was equipped with a bed and toilet. He was carrying computers, cameras, mobile phones, airport maps, and airport security passes for Canada, Thailand and Egypt.

With a dramatic increase in large and small container transport by sea,[11] the problem has grown, as these sealed containers often pass through ports without undergoing thorough checking[12] and are capable of containing anything from human terrorist cargo to arms and ammunition. It has been reported that one of Bin Laden's cargo freighters unloaded supplies in Kenya for the suicide cadres who subsequently bombed the US embassies in Kenya and Tanzania.[13]

In this context the new CSI (Container Security Initiative) is a step toward overcoming this challenge. However the CSI does not cover any port in the Indian Ocean at present (Durban, South Africa, and Colombo, Sri Lanka, are expected to join soon, along with Kelang, Malaysia, and Tanjung Priok, Indonesia).[14] In addition, many smaller host nations regard the initiative as an impediment to normal trade and a method of re-enforcing trade barriers.

Several terrorist organizations in and around the Indian Ocean are known to possess merchant fleets of various types. The Liberation Tigers of Tamil Eelam (LTTE), for example, have an entire flotilla engaged in dubious maritime trade. Most of these are registered under flag of convenience (FOC) countries known as "pan-ho-lib," i.e. Panama, Honduras and Liberia,[15] and are difficult to track as they routinely change names and registry. Lloyds of London lists 11 merchant ships belonging to Asian front companies that are in reality managed by Kumaran Pathmanathan of the LTTE.[16]

Thus FOCs pose another major challenge to maritime security. Flying the flag of a state other than the country of ownership enables the owners to avoid high registration fees and taxes, and to employ cheap labor operating under sub-standard conditions. It is estimated that there are about 30 such registries (some in private hands operating on behalf of states) mainly run by small island or impoverished nations.[17] Since the checks and balances introduced by these registries are undeniably lax, there is no guarantee as to the type of crew or the type of cargo that these ships carry.

Such ships are considered the safest bet for carrying out terrorist-related activities.

During the last few decades, several terrorist groups have mushroomed across the globe. Notwithstanding the fact that the sea is a complex medium, and requires great mastery to conduct attacks, these groups have developed significant capability to conduct attacks at sea, under the sea and more recently from the sea. Nearly two dozen terrorist groups have been identified as having engaged in acts of terrorism at sea and have struck in Latin America, Europe, the Middle East, South Asia and South-East Asia.[18]

Significantly, the terrorist groups have kept pace with modern navigation technologies and developed innovative tactics to challenge maritime forces. They have successfully attacked a range of targets, from poorly secured platforms such as oil tankers and ferries to making forays against highly defended warships, port infrastructure and oil terminals. Besides lethal weaponry, some terrorist groups have carried out attacks by employing marine leisure equipment (scuba diving equipment and diving apparatus, sea scooters, speedboats and tourist submarines) and devices and explosives that have commercial use. These items are all easy to acquire without inviting suspicion, and can be effortlessly deployed at sea and underwater. There are fears that terrorists may smuggle an unsophisticated nuclear or radiological device into a ship or transport it by container and detonate it in a port, creating a doomsday scenario.

The symbiotic relationship between gunrunning and drug trafficking is well known. It is extremely difficult to control one without controlling the other. Gunrunning by sea is by far the safest means for transferring arms and ammunition around the world, while drug trafficking is most lucrative. Insurgent movements around the world, like the United Wa State Army (UWSA) - a splintered faction of the Burmese Communist Party- operating from the northern Shan state in Myanmar - depend extensively on drug money to fuel their movement and equip their forces.

The LTTE has a vast and well-established network for gunrunning, with its reach extending as far as Japan. Their arms mostly originate in Cambodia, and are later loaded into small fishing trawlers from the port of Ranong in southern Thailand. This arms cargo is then transferred to bigger ships (often in mid-ocean), which transport the consignment to Sri Lanka. The seizure in a boat yard in Singapore of an incomplete submersible bound for the LTTE displays the extent of arms that are being transported illegally.

Bangladesh's capture of several small fishing craft laden with arms during the last few years has led to the conclusion that a lot of these arms also make their way from Thailand to the Cox Bazaar in Bangladesh. Similarly, the Royal Thai Navy's seizure of arms meant for the People's Liberation Army (Manipur) off the port of Ranong in 1997 clearly demonstrates the close nexus between arms trafficking and insurgent groups. The other major pipeline for Cambodian weapons is through Southern Thailand, and from there across the Malacca Straits to Aceh.[19]

There are clear links between the narcotics and illegal light weapons trade that include shared supply and transit routes, the use of weapons for protection amongst drug traffickers themselves, and funding of gunrunning through drug trade and vice versa.[20]

The other main source of insecurity relates to the rise of new naval powers in the Indian Ocean. While piracy and terrorism in the Indian Ocean are current issues, so-called Great Power rivalry is not yet an immediate security threat in the region. However, the potential effects of Great Power rivalry are more fundamental and reach further than acts of terrorism or piracy. In terms of this rivalry, two major issues stand out. The first is increasing maritime rivalry between India and China. Tensions between these two Asian powers have existed since the 1959 exile of the Dalai Lama to India, and the 1962 Sino–Indian border war. Moreover, China is a close security partner of Pakistan, which traditionally has a troubled relationship with India. Now that China and India are emerging as major powers, the Indian Ocean has ecome an additional area of potential tensions between the two. This is especially the case since 2009, when the Chinese navy started operations in the Indian Ocean in response to Somali piracy. For this purpose, China has so far maintained a continuous naval presence in the Gulf of Aden, on a rotating basis, with task forces consisting of two warships and one supply vessel. The warships carry Chinese special forces, which can provide onboard protection for commercial vessels. China has so far dispatched seventeen consecutive counter-piracy task forces to the Gulf of Aden.[21] Meanwhile, the steady rise of India as an economic power provides it with a growing capacity to play a role in the maritime domain. The Indian navy commenced counter-piracy operations in the Gulf of Aden in 2008,[22] and is speeding up its modernization and expansion of its capabilities in the maritime domain. The recent Indian purchase of twelve P-81 anti-submarine warfare aircraft from the United States is illustrative of this.[23]

The Chinese navy operates without bases in the region. Instead, Chinese navy ships are replenished through visits to various commercial ports around the western Indian Ocean. Logistical support at the local level is provided by Chinese companies.[24] Nonetheless, India seems concerned about the possibility of an increased Chinese naval presence in the future at sea and in places such as the Seychelles, which are often mentioned in international media as a potential location for a Chinese naval supply facility.[25] Moreover, China has close diplomatic and economic ties with a large number of littoral states in East Africa, the Middle East, South Asia, and South-East Asia. China has sold arms to many of these nations, and has invested in port construction in countries such as Pakistan, Myanmar, Sri Lanka and Bangladesh. Chinese shipping firms and commercial port operators are highly active in and along the Indian Ocean, and Chinese fishing and offshore oil and gas activities in the region are also increasing.

India's efforts to expand its navy and its ties with other littoral states are driven in part by the aim of keeping up with the growing Chinese presence in Indian Ocean. China's range of maritime activity extends even further west than the Indian Ocean. In 2011, a Chinese warship was present in the Mediterranean Sea to assist in the evacuation of Chinese citizens from Libya during its civil war.

A Chinese state-owned company, Cosco, is currently engaged in container port management in Greece,[26] and in the eastern Mediterranean the Chinese navy is escorting ships engaged in the chemical disarmament of Syria, operating from Cyprus.

The second major instance of potential Great Power rivalry in the Indian Ocean relates to the risk of spillover effects from maritime tensions in the western Pacific Ocean, including the East and South China Seas.[27] Competition for regional leadership in East and South-East Asia between China and the United States is increasingly manifesting itself in maritime security issues. The zones of prime strategic importance of China and the United States overlap in the East and South China Seas. The United States maintains a significant military presence in Japan and South Korea, with which it has security alliances. This presence includes the Japan-based Seventh Fleet. Other US security allies and partners in East and South-East Asia include the Philippines, Thailand, Singapore and Taiwan. The United States has also strengthened its security cooperation with Vietnam and Indonesia.

In recent years the United States has responded to China's rising influence by strengthening its military, diplomatic and economic efforts throughout the region. Closely intertwined with the Sino–US rivalry are security tensions between China and Japan. To an important degree, these revolve around conflicting territorial claims in the East China Sea, and Chinese naval activity close to Japanese territory. Given the role of the United States as Japan's ally and the heavy US military presence in Japan, the Sino–Japanese security relationship cannot be seen as separate from the Sino–US relationship. This high degree of interconnectedness relates also to the South China Sea. On the one hand, the supply lines of Japan and other US security partners are vulnerable to China's military influence in the South China Sea. On the other hand, China's own supply lines crossing the very same region are vulnerable to the military influence of the United States. In the South China Sea the US is indirectly involved in a territorial dispute between its ally, the Philippines, and China.

Although the US navy recently began stationing warships in Singapore, there have been no major signs so far that the maritime tensions in the East and South China seas are spilling over into the Indian Ocean. Nevertheless, not only China but also the US and Japan have a naval presence in the Indian Ocean. For decades, the United States has been the leading naval power in this region, with a military presence in the Persian Gulf and on the small island of Diego Garcia. During the 1990s, the US strengthened its naval presence in the region by establishing the Bahrain-based Fifth Fleet, which comprises an aircraft carrier strike group and multiple other task forces. The United States also oversees several combined naval task forces in the Indian Ocean, in which allies and security partners of the US participate. In addition, the US also has a presence through the North Atlantic Treaty Organization (NATO). One of the Combined Maritime Taskforces (CTF151) and a NATO naval operation (Ocean Shield) are aimed at counter-piracy operations in the Gulf of Aden.

The current Japanese naval presence in the Indian Ocean dates from 2001, when the Japanese navy (known as the Japan Maritime Self-Defence Force or JMSDF) commenced missions in the Indian Ocean under Operation Enduring Freedom–Maritime Interdiction Operation, a part of the US-led war on terror.[28] Until 2010, the JMSDF sent tankers to supply ships of the US-led coalition forces engaged in Afghanistan, as well as warships to join in operations to interdict weapons and drugs. Since 2009, the Japanese navy has been engaged in counter-piracy operations in the Gulf of Aden. The following year, the Japanese military established a *de facto* base in Djibouti to support its counter-piracy activities,[29] which are carried out by two destroyers and two P-3C maritime patrol aircraft.[30]

Although the United States, China, India and Japan all have a continuous naval presence in the western Indian Ocean, at present it seems unlikely that there will be a major naval arms race in that maritime region. While the United States is firmly entrenched and India is the emerging regional power,[31] in the short term neither China nor Japan are likely to have major force projection capabilities west of the Malacca Straits. Japan's military is constitutionally bound to focus on the defence of its own territory. Should Japan change (or re-interpret) its constitution in order to allow for collective defence, it would likely remain dependent on the United States to protect its supply lines in the Indian Ocean. China, on the other hand, does not yet have the military capabilities to be a dominant naval power in the Indian Ocean. Moreover, as pointed out by Chinese scholar Chu Shulong, in this context it would be futile for China to attempt to make its maritime supply routes across the Indian Ocean invulnerable to a blockade by the US navy.

Moreover, given China's long-standing policy of not establishing military bases abroad, it is possible that this will indeed remain the case in the Indian Ocean region in the near future. Still, China has major interests in the region, in particular its access to raw materials in the Middle East and Africa, and to markets there and in Europe. Beijing may therefore be expected to continue its present policy of building up strong diplomatic and economic influence throughout the Indian Ocean's littoral states. It is also likely that the Chinese military will continue to develop its regional presence in the sphere of non-traditional security. In the past two decades, China has participated in UN Peacekeeping Missions by sending non-combat troops. China recently upgraded its involvement in African peace operations by dispatching security forces tasked with protecting the UN mission's headquarters in Mali.

India's maritime security challenges cover the entire range from low intensity conflict and piracy, all the way to major-power strategic contests. Given its distinctive geography and the shift of global maritime focus from the Atlantic-Pacific combine to the Indo-Pacific continuum, the importance of the Indian Ocean Region in India's national security calculus has greatly increased in the post-Cold War era. Maritime security of India comprised of seaborne trade and infrastructure for its pursuit, management of sea resources, environmental issues and employment of naval forces.

Increased activity throughout the Indian Ocean region due to expanding regional and global trade in goods, ideas, people, and resources has raised a new set of maritime security challenges. Historical state-based concerns such as geopolitical fragility, internal political upheaval, insurgency, inter-state tensions, sea-lane security, and territorial disputes are now coupled with growing threats from non-state sources and asymmetric risks. Among these are growing risks from non-state actors including piracy, terrorism, and trafficking; the impacts of environmental degradation, resource depletion, climate change, and natural disasters; and weak states and failing institutions. These diverse challenges confront an equally diverse set of nations bordering this region. Such diversity in interests and capabilities saddles the region with political tensions and brings with it a greater danger of instability and conflict.

The energy thirsty nations such as China, India and other developing countries have no choice but to import large quantities of energy resources from around the world specially, West Asia. The dependence on the seas to get energy products to sustain their economies is growing progressively. This also brings in the threat of these vessels and products being targeted by both pirates and non-state actors. Chinese units while proceeding for anti-piracy patrols or while returning will plan for engaging the neighbouring navies of India in naval exercises that would gradually witness enhanced bilateral/multilateral exercises. The challenge for South Asia and particularly India is to manage the Chinese advances in to the Indian Ocean. The devastating effect of '2004 Tsunami' and other climate change effects are bigger threats for the region specially India. In the traditional security domain, the two incidents of shooting of fishermen in the EEZ of India by an Italian Tanker in 2013 and another shooting by a US ship USS Rappahannock in the waters of Dubai on July last year, bring out dimensions of security challenges as they impinge on normal fisheries and livelihood issues. In both the cases which resulted in the death of innocent Indians, it appears that the guards/crew did not assess the situation correctly and misinterpreted the action as that of pirates/suicide attackers.

The period after the defeat of the LTTE has seen increased incidence of the Indian fishermen coming in to conflict with their counter parts in Sri Lanka and also with the SL Navy. There have been allegations and counter allegations about use of excessive force and even fire arms to prevent fishermen from poaching. From the Indian fishermen point of view, historically, the contested waters belonged to India and they have every right to fish in the traditional waters. Having demarcated the maritime boundary with Sri Lanka in 1974, wherein, Kachchativu was gifted to Sri Lanka, the Indian fishermen have been debarred from fishing around that rich fishing grounds around that Island leading to skirmishes and incidents. It is not that only Indian fishermen are guilty of trespassing, the Indian Ocean has witnessed intrusions by fishermen of Pakistan, Bangladesh, Thailand, Myanmar and Sri Lanka who do cross into each other's territory while looking for fish. This will remain a great challenge with security overtones.

Conclusion

There are some serious issues such as Piracy, Terrorism, Safety of mercantile marine trade, proliferation, security of Straits, environmental protection that require deft handling. All these demand great attention to see that India and other stake holders work out strategies to ensure a peaceful environment in the Indian Ocean Region. If India is to fulfil its role as the 'net security provider in the Indian Ocean' and its ambitions as a regional maritime power, the vulnerabilities of its maritime security architecture, cruelly exposed in a series of recent accidents, must be addressed.

References

1. Panikkar, Kavalam Madhava, India and the Indian Ocean: An Essay on the Influence of Sea Power on Indian History (London: G. Allen & Unwin), 1945.
2. Ibid.
3. Potgieter, Thean, Maritime Security in the Indian Ocean: Strategic Setting and Features', ISS paper 236 (Pretoria: Institute for Security Studies, August), 2012.
4. Winner, Andrew C., Patricia Schneider, and Awet T. Weldemichael (2012), 'Maritime Terrorism and Piracy in the Indian Ocean Region', Journal of the Indian Ocean Region 8/2, 2012, p. 107.
5. Ginkel, Bibi van, and Frans-Paul van der Putten, 'Introduction: The International Response to Somali Piracy', in Bibi van Ginkel and Frans-Paul van der Putten, The International Response to Somali Piracy: Challenges and Opportunities (Leiden: Martinu Nijhoff), 2010, pp.1–12.
6. Edward Hanlon Jr, "Taking the Long View: Littoral Warfare Challenges", in Richard H. Shultz Jr and Robert L. Pfaltzgraff Jr (eds.), The Role of Naval Forces in 21st Century Operations (Dulles, VA: Brassey's), 2000, pp. 156–157.

7. International Maritime Organisation, "Reports on Acts of Piracy and Armed Robbery against Ships- Annual Report 2002," dated 17 April 2003, available in pdf at *http//www.imi.org.*

8. MV Alondra Rainbow, a 7,000-ton Panama-registered vessel belonging to Japanese owners was hijacked. The vessel was en route from Kuala Tanjung, Indonesia to Milkein Japan. The Piracy Reporting Center of the International Maritime Bureau had announced through a worldwide broadcast that pirates had captured the vessel. After a high-speed chase and drama it was finally captured by Indian Naval ship INS Praha.r

9. "Hunt for 20 terror ships", The *Observer International*, London, December 23, 2001.

10. "Inside the Ring", *http://www.gertzfile.com/ring010402.html.*

11. 'Containerisation',*www.choicegroup.co.in/html/cntrzation.htm.*

12. According to United States custom authorities, only 2 per cent of the cargo containers that enter seaports each day are inspected as cited in "Port of Entry Now Means Point of Anxiety," The New York Times, December 23, 2001.

13. "U.S. Ports Represent Weakness in Nation's Defenses, Analyses Shows," *http://www.military.com/Content/More Content/1,12044,FL_ports_103001,00.html*

14. "Container Security Initiative" at United States Customs and Border Protection website:*http://www.cbp.gov/xp/cgov/enforcement/international_activities/csi/.*

15. "Killing Of Sea Bird Not A Big Blow to LTTE Shipping Operations", The Sunday Times, February 1996.

16. Ibid.

17. "What are FOCs: A brief guide to flags of convenience", *www.itf.org.uk/seafarers/foc/Body_foc.html.*

18. Gunaratna, Rohan, "The Asymmetric Threat from Maritime Terrorism", Jane's Navy International, Vol. 106, No. 8, October 2001, p. 26.

19. David Capie "Small Arms Production Transfers in South East Asia," Canberra Papers on Strategy and Defence No.146, 2002, p. 20.

20. Research Report on "Combating Illicit Light Weapons Trafficking: Developments and Opportunities,"British American Security Information Council, London January 1998.

21. *http://english.peopledaily.com.cn/90783/8585823.html.*

22. *http://indiannavy.nic.in/operations/anti-piracy-operations.*

23. Tanchum, Micha'el, 'India Advances in Naval Arms Race with China', BESA Center Perspectives Paper 233, 14 January, 2014

24. Kamerling, Susanne, and Frans-Paul van der Putten, 'An Overseas Naval Presence without Oerseas Bases: China's Counter-piracy Operation in the Gulf of Aden', Journal of Current Chinese Affairs, 2011, pp. 119–146.

25. *http://www.washingtontimes.com/news/2013/jul/11/inside-china-chinese-navy-courts-seychelles/?page = all.*

26. Van der Putten, Frans-Paul, 'Chinese Investment in the Port of Piraeus, Greece: The Relevance for the EU and the Netherlands', Report (The Hague: Clingendael), 14 February, 2014.

27. Sweijs, Tim, 'The Maritime Future of the Indian Ocean: Putting the G Back into Great Power Politics', Future, Isse 13 (The Hague: HCSS), 25 October, 2010.

28. Yoshihara, Toshi, and James R. Holmes, 'Don't Expect Much from Japan in the Indian Ocean', Journal of Military and Strategic Studies 13/2, winter, 2011, p. 20.

29. Kato, Yoichi, 'SDF's New Anti-Piracy Base Creates Dilemma', Pacific Forum CSIS, 25 August, 2011.

30. *http://www.mofa.go.jp/policy/piracy/ja_somalia.html*

31. India International Centre, 'Maritime Security Challenges in the Indian Ocean Region: A Workshop Report' (New Delhi: IIC), 23–24 February 2011.

3

India's Maritime Interests in The Indian Ocean

The growing strategic and economic importance of the Indian Ocean has significant relevance for the rise of India. With the rising indices of maritime trade and growing naval power, India will seek to maintain its long-term presence in the Indian Ocean. India is the pivot state of the Indian Ocean region. Its historical-civilizational past, its geo-strategic location, its past maritime economic trade linkages with West Asia and East Asia have resulted in the prominence of the Indian Ocean as an ancient civilizational legacy.[1]

India's interests are strategic and proximate. As one of the largest countries in the region, and geographically located as it is, India has responsibilities in ensuring security of the commons, as well as legitimate concerns. The Indian Ocean is becoming increasingly important to India's economic and security interests. The geo strategic importance of Indian Ocean increased during the cold war period. But with the end of cold war the geopolitical importance of the area has multiplied with Asia replacing Europe as the new theatre of international politics and diversifying itself.[2] The Indian

Ocean region occupies a crucial importance, especially because of the presence of major powers in the region and potential of the regional powers to form the center stage for the challenges in the 21st century. In the contemporary time, the Indian Ocean is not only important because of the great powers' economic and military interests but it is also vulnerable due to organized network of global terrorism, piracy, human smuggling, drug trafficking, drug smuggling and gun running, as well as proliferation of munitions between and among insurgent groups.[3]

Since the ancient history, maintaining of a maritime domain became an important factor to India. India is at the heart of the Indian Ocean and constitutes the junction between the eastern and the western rim. India as a rising global power in the twenty-first century believes Indian Ocean to be its sphere of influence and seeks to play a crucial role in ensuring lasting security in the Ocean, thereby serving its strategic interests. *Indian Maritime Doctrine* of 2004, 2009 and *India's Maritime Military Strategy* of 2007 reflect a shift of maritime vision from a small coastal-hugging passive brown water fleet to a larger ocean-going active blue water fleet capable of power projection throughout the Indian Ocean. Indian Ocean has been projected as the area of primary strategic interest for India. To this end, the Indian Navy has a crucial role to play.[4] India's policy towards the Indian Ocean region has been shaped by the twin objective of contributing to the world peace and securing its own vital interests in the region. The geographical location of the country at the centre of the ocean makes its security, commerce and trade all dependent on the preservation of stability in the region. India is a country with rich maritime tradition spanning over 4,000 years.[5]

India has developed long-term strategic and economic interests in the Indian Ocean. Former India's Prime Minister, Atal Bihari Vajpayee made the following statement on India's strategic priorities during the Combined Commanders' Conference in November 2003 that,

> '...the strategic frontiers of today's India, grown in international stature, have expanded well beyond confines of South Asia...Our security environment ranges from Persian Gulf to Straits of Malacca across the Indian Ocean, includes Central Asia and Afghanistan, China...and South- East Asia. Our strategic thinking has also to extend to these horizons.'[6]

Given India's critical dependence on the Indian Ocean for its trade and commerce, its natural situational advantages, its maritime potential, and robust presence, there is a common understanding that India should and must aspire to "emerge as the leader with an overarching influence in the region" and be "the catalyst for peace, stability and tranquillity". Therefore, maritime security is receiving ever greater attention in Indian strategic thinking as India is aspiring for great power status.[7]

Former Naval Chief, Admiral Arun Prakash has noted that, "India's national objective lies in ensuring a secure and stable environment which will permit the economic development and social uplift of its masses, so that the country can ultimately take its rightful place in the international comity of nations. Within this overall objective our primary maritime interest is to ensure national security and provide insulation from external interference, so that the vital task of fostering economic growth and undertaking development activities can take place in a secure environment."[8] Indian interest in the Indian Ocean region is quite understandable as any sort of security concerns about instability that characterises and destabilises the region would definitely have significant implications on our country. The other reasons could be the region's vital role in oil production and its importance for energy shipments, the wealth of resources and raw materials in the region, involvement of extra-regional powers in a number of conflicts, and the rise of new regional powers and their ability to project their power.

The Indian ambitions in the Indian Ocean can be reflected from the very fact that it holds 65 per cent of strategic raw minerals and 31 per cent of gas, comprises 30 per cent of the world population and is characterised by fast-growing economies and a large consumer market.[9] Since India rely on sea to fulfill its 89 percent of oil requirements. It is being the major stakeholder in Indian Ocean trade and commerce activities in respect of imported crude oil, raw materials, and consumer goods, the country's exports. In this context, it becomes necessary for India to ensure the security of SLOCs from the Persian Gulf, Europe, and East Asia. The security of these vital shipping lanes is also linked with India's dependence on the security of the Indian Ocean, combined with its need to monitor and, if necessary, check the naval activity of other regional powers.

The Indian Navy's presence has touched to 40 ships and submarines, two nuclear submarines, two aircraft carriers. This would go up to have a 165-ship fleet by 2022 ranging from surface combatants, submarines to three aircraft carrier groups with a total of 400 MiG-29K aircraft and helicopters. Sanjay Chaturvedi, an expert in maritime security and Indian Ocean is of the view that, 'This would result in the change of balance of power in the Indian Ocean, with a tilt decisively in India's favour.'[10] Donald Berlin, professor at the Asia-Pacific Center for Security Studies in Honolulu, and an expert in maritime strategic issues has observed this evolving role of India in the IOR: New Delhi regards the Indian Ocean as its back yard and deems…that India functions as, eventually, the predominant influence in this region…In the expansive view of many Indians, India's security perimeter should extend from the Strait of Malacca to the Strait of Hormuz and from the coast of Africa to the Western shores of Australia."[11] The present chapter seeks to examine India's maritime interests and power in the context of the growing significance of Indian Ocean. In doing so, the chapter first highlight the geo-strategic location of India in the context of Indian Ocean maritime security. Then it discusses the geo-strategic significance of Indian Ocean for India. Further, it analyses India's maritime power in the twenty-first century.

India's Geo-Strategic Location

Before dwelling on the India's strategic interests in the Indian Ocean, it is imperative that the geo-strategic location of India in the context of Indian Ocean maritime security be explained first. India is located strategically in the Indian Ocean region. India's geographical location represents a significant point in the Indian Ocean region. Without any doubt, the geo-strategic location of India generates potential geopolitical advantages for India in Indian Ocean. K.M. Panikkar has opined that, 'The vital feature which differentiates the Indian Ocean from the Atlantic or the Pacific is the subcontinent of India, which juts out far into the sea for a thousand miles. It is the geographical position of India that changes the character of the Indian Ocean.' While the then Indian Foreign Secretary, Nirupama Rao has underlined in 2010 that 'India and the Indian Ocean are inseparable. In the midst of the third largest ocean in the world, India's location is in many ways her destiny'. India's naval leadership talks of 'leveraging our strategic geography ... by virtue of India's geo-strategic location in the Indian Ocean'.[12]

Indian Maritime Doctrine of 2004 has underlined that,

> "India sits astride ... major commercial routes and energy lifelines crisscrossing the Indian Ocean region. Outlying Indian possessions such as the Andaman and Nicobar islands sit athwart the approaches to the Strait of Malacca, while the Persian Gulf is near India's western coastline, conferring a measure of influence

over vital sea communications to and from what amounts to a bay in the Indian Ocean. While geography may not be destiny, the document states bluntly that "by virtue of our geography, we are . . . in a position to greatly influence the movement/security of shipping along the SLOCs in the [Indian Ocean Region] provided we have the maritime power to do so. Control of the choke points could be useful as a bargaining chip in the international power game, where the currency of military power remains a stark reality."[13]

Map 3.1

Geo-Strategic Location of India in Indian Ocean

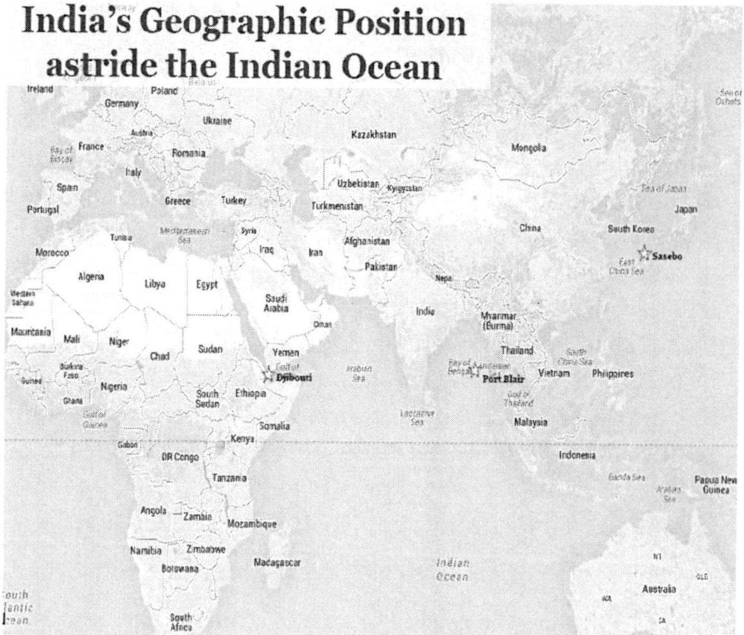

Source: This Map is adopted from the Power Point Presentation made by Indian Ambassador Hemant Krishan Singh on 'Regional Security: The View From New Delhi', at the 12th India-Korea Dialogue, New Delhi, 24-25 October 2013.

India shares maritime boundaries not just with three South Asian neighbours but also with three nations of South East Asia - Myanmar, Thailand and Indonesia; there is close proximity with a fourth, Malaysia. India is centrally located between the East and Western stretches of the Indian Ocean, thereby able to deploy maritime sea power in both directions more easily than other littoral states that are found in one half or the other of the Indian Ocean. India also juts southwards deep into the Indian Ocean, with a long coastline of just over 4,670 miles. This is an immediate asset for Indian Ocean operations, and magnifies India power projection much further than is the case for other states huddling along the northern littoral of the Indian Ocean. Therefore, it won't be wrong to put forth an argument that, 'India's strategic location in the Indian Ocean ... bestows upon us a natural ability to play a leading role in ensuring peace and stability in the Indian Ocean Region.'[14]

India with a coastline of over 7,500 Kms is bordered by the sea on three sides - Arabian Sea on the west, Indian Ocean in the south and the Bay of Bengal to the east. The Andaman & Nicobar Islands located 1300 km away from the nearest point on our East coast assume strategic predominance with respect to the entrance to the Malacca Straits. In the Arabian Sea, the Lakshadweep and Minicoy islands, situated on the sea-lanes of communication running eastwards from the Persian Gulf and the Red sea are 450 km away from the nearest point on the West coast. This way we can say that India is both a maritime as well as a continental entity.

Among the Indian Ocean littoral states, India occupies an important position by virtue of two flash points of the Indian Ocean-one, the Persian Gulf Region which has abundant oil resources and secondly, the Strait of Malacca located strategically across the international oceanic trade route between Far East and the European and the Indian

Ocean littoral states.[15] With a coastline of over 7,500 Kms and an Exclusive Economic Zone of 2.1 million Sq. Kms, India's maritime resources are enormous and can be exploited towards securing food and energy security. India at present has several major ports and intermediate ports plus minor ports along its coastline.

Geo-Strategic Significance of Indian Ocean for India

The statement made by former Indian Foreign Secretary Nirupama Rao clearly reflects the close linkage between India and Indian Ocean that, 'India and the Indian Ocean are inseparable. In the midst of the third largest ocean in the world, India's location is in many ways her destiny'.[16] The significance of Indian Ocean for India is manifold. From the Political, economic and strategic perspective, Indian Ocean holds immense significance for our country. Firstly, Trans Indian ocean routes which connect the countries of Europe in the West and the countries of East Asia which has helped India to encourage multilateralism through regional organizations like ASEAN, APEC, IOR-ARC, BIMSTEC, SAARC and EAS. Secondly, this puts India in the ideal place to establish to be able to trade with West Asia, Africa and Europe from the Western coast and with the Southeast and East Asia from the Eastern coast. Thirdly, the long coastline and the natural harbors call for a proactive naval diplomacy in presence of militia groups. Fourthly, it has given India a distinct climate than the rest of the Asian Continent and has numerous ports of much distance due to which trade ships have to pass India which adds to her global strategic importance. Fifthly, the mutual perception of India and PRC will determine the future of Indian Ocean. It is the stage of unfolding Asian drama and India is to choose whether it will play the role of protagonist or not. Sixthly, the emerging concern for India is with regard environmentalism (tsunami in 2004) and corporatism (ONGC Videsh exploration near Vietnam).[17]

Conceptualising Maritime Security

Maritime security falls within the purview of national security. Maritime security is one part of the national security.[18] Like the concept of security, the concept of maritime security is faced with the problem of ambiguity. There is no such commonly accepted definition on maritime security. Different countries have defined the concept of maritime security depending upon the kinds of maritime threats they face. In simple word, we can say that maritime security is all about security the nation from danger arising in or from the sea. In other word, maritime security may be defined as "the all-encompassing complementary faction of national security of a maritime nation from an ocean specific terrain assessment applicable to that nation."

Traditionally, the concept of maritime security has been related to the role navies and defence forces play in protecting the nation and its national interests against sea borne threats primarily of a military nature. However, post 9/11 and in particular after 26/11 Mumbai attacks, the concept of maritime security has expanded and has acquired immense significance at the regional and global level. It is still about protecting national security but instead of overt threats from military forces, there is a new emphasis on asymmetric threats, including both maritime terrorism and piracy. This focus is apparent in the work of the International Maritime Organization (IMO) directed towards enhancing the security of international shipping and seaborne trade.[19]

According to renowned strategic analysts, Jasjit Singh, former director of Centre for Air Power Studies, the term 'maritime security' represents the broadest approach to issues and aspects which pertain to the sea and have an important bearing on the country's security. According to him the concept of maritime security goes well beyond the military aspect although military power and security remains the final arbiter of national security.[20] A Dalhousie University study has defined maritime security as "a process of maintaining stability in the international system on, over, under and from the sea."[21]

Maritime security is both multi-dimensional and multifaceted encompassing both military and non-military issues. The military security threats borne out of sea includes naval threats and challenges while, non-military threats includes arms trafficking, narco-terrorism, piracy, shipping, fishing, vulnerability of Sea Lanes of Communication (SLOC) and other illicit activities.[22] Countering these irregular and transnational threats enhances global stability, and secures freedom of navigation for the benefit of all nations. Maritime security benefit not only to a particular nation, but other maritime states gets the benefit out of it. Therefore, it requires cooperation rather than conflict to deal the sea-borne issues.

India as a Maritime Power

This section would dwell on the need for India to strengthen its maritime power in the 21st century. India possesses every potential to be strong maritime power in the changing maritime security environment. However, before going into the details on Indian maritime power, one would need to understand the concept of maritime power.

The honorable President of India, Shri. Pranab Mukherjee has noted that,

> '...a nation's social and economic well being is intricately linked to the seas, not only for trade but also how it faces threats to its own security that develop across the seas...our resolve to achieve high growth can be realised only if our maritime frontiers and assets are safe, stable and act as enablers. The Indian Navy, as the primary element of India's maritime power, has the challenging task of safeguarding the country's maritime interests."[23]

Former India's Chief of Naval Staff, Arun Prakash has

very rightly noted that, 'India's desired role of being the net provider of security in the IOR can only be sustained by growth in India's maritime capability.'[24] Maritime power is the ability of a nation to use the seas to safeguard and progress its national interests. As such, it is a pillar of national security policy and is a key enabler in the formulation and implementation of viable National and Military Strategies. The Navy is the prime instrument and manifestation of the maritime power of a nation-state. The *raison d'etre* (French phrase for 'reason for existence') of a navy is to safeguard the nation's use of seas for its legitimate sovereign purposes, whilst concurrently guarding against inimical use of the sea by others. Naval forces are capable of carrying out multifarious tasks due to their inherent and unique attributes. These enable the deployment of maritime forces in areas of interest without any constraints.[25]

Indian maritime power represents the only prudent response to strategic conditions that are at once promising and worrisome in economic terms. As India rises as a great power, it becomes imperative for India to develop itself as a maritime power in tune to the changing scenario. A modernised and capable naval force supports the expansion of India's reach into the Indian Ocean region, with which it has a deep historical, commercial and security linkages. The chapter argues that without developing adequate maritime strategy and power, New Delhi cannot attain the desired status in the global hierarchy.

As the premier maritime force in the region, India has both security concerns at sea and responsibility to ensure safe movement across the shipping routes of the IO which needs both capabilities and cooperative interfaces with others. India's destiny has always been intricately linked to the sea, and events in history testify the same. Right from ancient to medieval and modern history, every era of intense maritime activity has been associated with economic prosperity and political stability. India, with its over 7,500 km long coastline, cannot ignore its maritime dimension while formulating its national strategy.[26] India is a conventional and maritime power. India's regional maritime identity has undergone a major change during the past two decades. India now has become a regional maritime power.

Geographically, India occupies the central position in the Indian Ocean. It lays half way between Straits of Malacca and Hormuz the two most important waterways of the world. It has seven maritime neighbours. India is a sea going nation and very much dependant on maritime trade. Former Indian Naval Chief, Arun Prakash had observed that, 'As the pre-eminent maritime power in the Indian Ocean, we must possess and maintain a capability for sustained operations in our area of interest, including power projection.' Over the years, Indian military is the fast growing enterprise with acquisition of defence assets, gathering surveillance and shore-based arsenals, submarines and latest aircraft carriers with plans to revamp its naval forces which have built its maritime capability through garnering a piffling share of defence budget. Rationality paves way to assembling latest hi-tech weaponry alongside well-equipped and well-trained forces to combat piracy and guard the strategic interests, be it: security assurances to all littoral states or economic security of their unchecked flow of shipments.

In tune to its growing economic and military prowess, India has strengthened its maritime domain. India's regional maritime identity has undergone a major change during the past decades. In the context of changed international scenario, India has re-casted her policies to be a major maritime power by 2025. In the past two decades we have witnessed an impressive growth in this field. Now, India has become a regional maritime power by all means. Former Naval chief Admiral Arun Prakash has rightly pointed out, 'The Indian Navy is the largest and most capable resident navy in the

Indian Ocean Region, and is seen by most maritime powers as a stabilizing force. As India grows economically, our stake in the seas around us will also grow, and our maritime power will also increase commensurately.'

Besides, a country's merchant marine and its ports are equally important elements of its strength at sea. India has 13 major and 185 notified minor and intermediate sea ports. In order to gross weight tonnage conveyed annually, Bombay, Vishakhapatnam, Madras and Marmagoa are the most important ports in India. India has 7 shipyards (4 big and 3 medium) under the control of central government, 2 shipyard controlled by state governments, 35 privately owned shipyards and 18 dry docks for major ship repair needs. Now, India has become self sufficient in the field of ship building and repair of almost of all sizes. The Cochin Shipyard in Kochi, Hindustan Shipyard Ltd. (HSL) in Vishakhapatnam and Hooghly Dock and Port Engineers in Calcutta are the most important shipbuilding enterprises in India. In addition, India is the only country in the IOR, to have an operational knowledge of nuclear submarine.

Being the most important and responsible state of IOR, India's seeks to develop a maritime policy to manage and increase its maritime power steadily, so that no one can challenge its position in this region in future. India has initiated several measures in this direction during the past years.[27] India is the only Indian Ocean country with aspirations comparable to China to become a major maritime power. India's new naval posture is bolstered by an ambitious warship procurement that projects an expanded aircraft carrier and nuclear powered submarine. India is rapidly enlarging its navy. Three key acquisitions by Indian navy are long range aircraft, aircraft carriers and nuclear submarines, makes India a formidable force in Indian Ocean.[28] Indian naval perception towards China's growing presence in Indian Ocean must be supported by strengthening our own military capabilities.

India's Maritime Strategic Interest

The Indian Ocean is important to India for a variety of reasons that vary from economic to political and security-related concerns. The issues at stake for India are the protection of her long coastline, her island territories, and the trade routes through which her imports and exports pass. It has diverse economic maritime interests in the Indian Ocean and is naturally in line to adopt the leadership role in the IOR. Legitimate maritime growth is vital to our national interests and India will certainly carry forward its ongoing maritime activities with vigour and strategic prioritizing. Renowned Indian historian, KM Panikkar has made a spectacular assessment way back in the early 1940s, that 'the peninsular character of the country and the essential dependence of its trade on maritime traffic' would give Indian Ocean a preponderant influence on its destiny, and "the economic life of India will be completely at the mercy of the power which controls the seas". He also held that "India never lost her independence till she lost the command of the sea in the first decade of the sixteenth century", and thus the future of India would depend not on its land frontiers but "on the oceanic expanse which washes the three sides of India".

In March 1958, Prime Minister Nehru said, "I ponder over our close links with the sea and how the sea has brought us together. From time immemorial the people of India have had very intimate connections with the sea. ...We cannot afford to be weak at sea ... history has shown that whatever power controls the Indian Ocean has, in the first instance, India's seaborne trade at her mercy, and in the second, India's very independence itself".[29]

India has a vast and varied Maritime interest that needs to be furthered and protected. These interests include Energy Security, fisheries, mining, and maritime trade to name only a few. Equally vast and varied are the complex Maritime security threats and challenges. They span from terrorism and piracy to drug trafficking, gun running, illegal immigration, environmental pollution and movement of contraband. This way, we can say that India's maritime interests encompass both the exploitation of the sea resources such as off-shore hydrocarbon explorations under the nation's jurisdiction and the protection of national integrity ranging from military intervention, anti-terrorism and anti-piracy actions.

According to the *Indian Maritime Doctrine of 2004,*

> 'India's primary maritime interest is to assure national security. This is not restricted to just guarding the coastline and island territories, but also extends to safeguarding our interests in the [exclusive economic zone] as well as protecting our trade. This creates an environment that is conducive to rapid economic growth of the country. Since trade is the lifeblood of India, keeping our SLOCs [sea lines of communication] open in times of peace, tension or hostilities is a primary national maritime interest.'[30]

While inaugurating the chair For Maritime Studies and Research University of Calicut, Admiral Arun Prakash said, 'India's national objective lies in ensuring a secure and stable environment which will permit the economic development and social uplift of its masses, so that the country can ultimately take its rightful place in the international comity of nations. Within this overall objective our primary 'maritime interest is to ensure national security and provide insulation from external interference, so that the vital task of fostering economic growth and undertaking development activities can take place in a secure environment.'[31]

India maritime interests also lies in protecting its offshore oil and gas fields, ongoing deep-sea oil drilling projects in its vast exclusive economic zone, and an extensive infrastructure of shore and offshore oil and gas wells, ports and pipeline grids, and refineries. India's offshore oil assets are spread over an area of 48,000 sq. km. and are expected to double by 2015. Overseas trade, 95 per cent of which transits through the sea, is expected to cross $ 400 billion by 2010 and $ 1 trillion by 2020, when over 8000 tankers are expected to be touching Indian ports. With growing trade, mostly by sea, there is a proportionate increase in Indian liabilities towards the protection of shipping, off-shore assets and protection of Exclusive Economic Zone. Any laxity on the nation's part may cripple the economic lifeline of the nation.[32]

With India also rising economically and emerging as a major military power in the region with the impressive naval presence in the region things have changed. As the logic of globalization unfolded over the last two decades, Indian naval leadership began to invent a new maritime strategy that is in tune with the changed circumstances. The phrases from 'Aden to Malacca' from 'Suez to South China Sea' were injected into national discourse.[33] However, the Indian Navy's maritime doctrine of 2009 has very clearly made a distinction between the primary and security maritime interests of our country. The primary maritime interests include traditional maritime perspective such as the India's maritime zones, the Arabian Sea and the Bay of Bengal plus the Cape of Good Hope and the Mozambique Channel. The secondary areas of maritime interests has been expanded and more significant and much broader which includes South China Sea, other areas of West Pacific Ocean and friendly littoral countries located herein and other areas of national interests based on considerations of diaspora and overseas investment.[34]

A large volume of India's trade passes through the Gulf of Aden, estimated at about US$ 110 billion annually. About 24 Indian-flagged merchant ships transit the Gulf of Aden every month. Moreover, more than 6 percent of seafarers engaged in international shipping companies are Indian nationals. We, therefore, have a strong interest in ensuring the security of maritime traffic off the Somali coast, the Gulf of Aden and the Arabian Sea.[35] However, Vice Admiral Pradeep Chauhan, Western Naval Command during his talk on India's maritime Security and the Navy's transformational role at the observer research foundation in Mumbai has clearly spelt out the India's maritime interests and the role the Indian Navy has to play in ensuring maritime security as follows:

a. ensuring stability and security in India's maritime zones, maritime neighbourhood and other areas of maritime interest;

b. Preserve and project other national interests in the maritime dimension.

c. protection from all sorts of maritime related threats

d. Protect India's sovereignty and territorial integrity against threats in the maritime environment.

e. contributing to our energy security by ensuring the security of energy

f. protection and safety of overseas trade and our sea lines of communication

g. protection and sustainable exploitation of the resources of the EEZ

h. supporting scientific research, including that in Antarctica

i. provision of support and extrication options to the Indian diaspora.[36]

There is a more proximate dimension to India's security interests which is acquiring significance. According to H. K. Singh, India's maritime security interests require that its cooperation arrangements with neighbouring countries go beyond periodic cooperation to include inter-operability training and logistical support. To take full advantage of India's geographical location, its maritime security initiatives with these countries must extend across the wider Indian

Ocean region and include partnerships with Japan, Indonesia, Australia and the US.[37]

By ensuring maritime security India would be able to maintain and strengthen its command of the sea in the Indian Ocean so as to use this maritime domain to achieve key strategic objectives. Protecting India's maritime interests is the responsibility of the Indian Navy, which has emerged as the fifth largest Navy in the world transforming itself from a coastal defence force to a "three dimensional blue water force". The Navy has been tasked with the security of the sea lanes of communication, protection of the littoral states, fighting piracy in the Sea of Aden, Malacca Straits and the South China Sea, combating maritime terrorism, tackling maritime pollution and environmental disasters in the waters of the Indian Ocean.

Indian Ocean: An Energy Corridor

Energy security is another matter of concern for our country; India will continue to rely on Indian Ocean. Here energy security involves not just identifying sources but equally, its safe movement and handling. The country imports 70 per cent of its oil and gas annually and this figure will rise to over 80% in the next ten years. The number of tankers carrying these supplies to our ports is likely to increase from 4000 odd today to nearly 7500 by 2020. Safe movement of the ships at sea and speedy discharge of their cargoes in ports is vital. India also has offshore oil exploration and exploitation platforms on either coast spread across 50000 square kilometers and it is likely that this area may double in the next decade; platforms in these waters which process oil and gas are very valuable assets which need to be safe guarded. A related concern is the security of seaborne trade. The country's imports and exports have reached $ 500 billion already and may well touch $ 2 trillion by 2020. Almost all of this trade moves by sea, through the shipping routes and narrow channels mentioned earlier.

Any adverse effect on the safe movement of this trade will impact on economic growth.[38]

With energy pipelines still far from reality, and only a nascent civilian nuclear programme, India remains highly dependent on energy imports and increasingly seeks to secure shipping lanes for the transportation of oil, from Iran and Burma to as far abroad as Sudan and Nigeria. Nearly half of global seaborne trade passes through the Indian Ocean, around 40 per cent of offshore oil production comes from the Indian Ocean, and 65 per cent of the world's oil and 35 per cent of its gas reserves are found in the littoral states of the Ocean. This makes the region strategically important from India's energy and economic security.[39]

The Indian Ocean emerges as the bastion of world economy in the 21st century. Its maritime routes will fuel the economic engines of rising Asian powers like China and India, as well as that of the industrialised world. With the continuous economic development and political stability in Africa, the continent will offer further strategic impetus to Indian Ocean trading networks. Shielding energy networks in the maritime domain will, however, require a formidable naval presence vital for sea control. The Indian Ocean is of crucial strategic value due to its own oil reserves and those in the Persian Gulf. It not only serves as the world's most important energy and international trade maritime route but also a central theatre of naval manoeuvring for rival powers to augment their naval strength and forge alliances to offset the opposing side.

The Indian Ocean harbours an array of non-energy, renewable and nonrenewable resources. According to estimates, between now and 2025, the world's leading economies would continue to depend on traditional energy reserves. "Oil and Liquefied Natural Gas (OLNG) are the two with inherent naval significance, as they must be transported by sea." Being cheaper than any overland substitutes, maritime transport stands as the ideal choice to transport energy goods. The Indian Ocean has the world's largest concentration of littorals rich in oil and gas reserves. "The region boasts 80 per cent of the world's proven oil reserves and 17 per cent of natural gas. 40 per cent of global seaborne commerce moves across the ocean, one-fifth of which comprises oil and gas. Each day, over 25 million barrels of oil transits through the Strait of Hormuz to key importers like the US, China, France, India and Japan." The growing unrest in South and Central Asia has left the security of overland pipelines extremely uncertain thereby increasing the dependence on sea transportation.[40]

India as a Net Security Provider in the Indian Ocean

Since Indian Ocean form the key to India's maritime calculus and a crucial component of its national security, India will seek to play the role a net security provider in the Indian Ocean. India's dependence on the security of the Indian Ocean, combined with its need to monitor and, if necessary, check the naval activity of other regional powers, has driven the country to reach out deep into the ocean, far beyond its own littoral to enable more expansive maritime domain awareness (MDA), develop basing opportunities, and fortify naval operational and diplomatic ties. Currently, India has close naval ties with Mozambique, Mauritius, and the Seychelles, having donated patrol vessels to both of the latter countries. As part of its MDA expansion program, the Indian navy has also established a radio and radar monitoring station on Madagascar, and has long maintained monitoring capabilities in the Nicobar Islands that sit astride shipping routes leading to and from Malacca. The extension of the Indian navy's ability to monitor the IOR has been driven in no small part by China's steadily expanding commercial and maritime ties with Bangladesh, Iran, Kenya, Myanmar, Pakistan, Seychelles, and Sri Lanka.[41]

The 'net security provider' concept emerged during the

2009 'Shangri La Dialogue', when the then US Secretary of Defence Mr Robert Gates stated,

> "When it comes to India, we have seen a watershed in our relations – cooperation that would have been unthinkable in the recent past... In coming years, we look to India to be a partner and net provider of security in the Indian Ocean and beyond."

Further in the 2010 in the US '*Quadrennial Defense Review*' (QDR), it was predicted that,

> "India's military capabilities are rapidly improving through increased defense acquisitions, and they now include long-range maritime surveillance, maritime interdiction and patrolling, air interdiction, and strategic airlift. India has already established its worldwide military influence through counterpiracy, peacekeeping, humanitarian assistance, and disaster relief efforts. As its military capabilities grow, India will contribute to Asia as a net provider of security in the Indian Ocean and beyond."[42]

During the Naval Commanders Conference held in New Delhi on 26 October 2015, the Indian Defence Minister Shri Manohar Parrikar released India's revised maritime-military strategy titled, 'Ensuring Secure Seas: Indian Maritime Security Strategy' (IMSS-2015). The IMSS – 2015 clearly pointed out the fact that India's role as a 'net maritime security provider' in the region is not only its normative responsibility as a regional power, but is also closely interwoven with the nation's own economic growth and prosperity. The 'roadmap' in IMSS-2015 provides a direction to the Navy to play this role as an effective instrument of the nation's proactive foreign policy, in consonance with the ongoing endeavour of its apex political leadership, and echoes the enunciation of Prime Minister Narendra Modi's vision of "SAGAR" (Security and Growth for All in the Region). However, it remains to be seen how India's navy would effectively balance the rather conflicting national security priorities of ensuring territorial defence across its oceanic frontiers versus providing 'net maritime security' in its regional neighbourhood.[43]

While underlying the role of India as a security provider in the Indian Ocean, Indian Naval Chief, Admiral D.K. Joshi, in a speech at IDSA on 5 March 2013 has noted that,

> 'India's geo-strategic location positions us right at the confluence of major arteries of world trade. The Indian Navy is therefore viewed by some of the littorals as a suitable agency to facilitate regional maritime security in the IOR as a net security provider.'[44]

As usual, the Indian Navy will seek to pursue a proactive engagement with the coastal and small island nations in the Indian Ocean region and ensure peace and stability to meet its wider security interests. Indian Navy has so far shown its commitment to ensure peace and security in the region by way of close engagement with the island nations. It has patrolled Mauritius EEZ since 2003 and deputes a naval officer to manage the National Coast Guard of Mauritius. In addition to this, it has provided three Dornier 228 maritime surveillance aircraft in the year 2004 and 2010 plus three new Islander aircraft engines in 2013 and even a coastal surveillance radar system. Indian Navy and Coast Guard also assist Seychelles in maintaining security b providing maritime surveillance, ocean surveys, training and maritime military equipment and repair.

Other than these, Indian Navy has played a crucial role in securing the Sea Lanes of Communications (SLOCs) in the Indian Ocean. In the post 9/11 attacks in United States, India has agreed to escort the sensitive US cargos through the Straits of Malacca. Besides, Indian Navy has played a crucial a significant role in counter-piracy operations off-Somalia over the last many years (more details on the Indian effort in anti-piracy operations can be seen in chapter 4). [45] The former Defence Minister of India Shri. A.K. Antony told on the occasion of 2012 Naval Chiefs Conference that 'India's strategic location in the Indian Ocean and the professional capability of our Navy bestows upon us a natural ability to play a leading role in ensuring peace and stability in the Indian Ocean Region'.[46]

Table 3.1

Indian Naval Capability in the Indian Ocean

Platform	No.	Class/Type
Aircraft Carrier	1	Viraat class (Sea Harrier)
Submarines	14	Shishumar & Sindhughosh class
Destroyers	8	Delhi and Rajput class
Frigates	13	Shivalik, Talwar, Brahmaputra, Godavari, and Giri class
Corvettes	8	Khukri and Giri class
Offshore/ASW patrol vessels	10	Kora and Sukanya class
Minesweepers	9	Pondicherry/Karwar class
Missile boats	12	Veer class
Amphibious ships	11	Magar, Kumbhir class, and LCUs
Auxiliary tankers	3	Jyoti, Aditya, and Deepak
Future ships, Submarines, and aviation		Vikrant class and Vikramaditya class aircraft carriers; Kolkata class destroyers; Talwar class frigates; Scorpiene class conventional submarines and Akula II nuclear attack submarines; and MiG-29 K/KUB fighters for aircraft carriers

Source: Rupert Herbert-Burns, "Naval Power in the Indian Ocean: Evolving Roles, Missions and Capabilities", in David Michel and Russell Sticklor (eds.), *Indian Ocean Rising: Maritime Security and Policy Challenges* (Washington: Stimson, July 2012), p. 49.

Conclusion

From the above analysis, it can be suggested that India's Geo-strategic location in the Indian Ocean would be of great significance in the 21st century world where Asian balance of power would be of critical relevance. India sits astride some of the most crucial sea-lanes of the world. Indian Ocean is home to nearly 70 per cent of the maritime traffic of the world. India's own maritime interests are enormous.

India should maintain a strong maritime force to safeguard her long term national interests, which lie increasingly in the oceans. With India's ever-growing reliance on imported energy, any disruptions in the Indian Ocean (which are particularly feasible at "choke points" such as the Strait of Hormuz, the Gulf of Aden, the Suez Canal and the Strait of Malacca), can lead to serious consequences for the Indian economy. The economic well-being of our country depends greatly upon the trade and commerce that pass through the oceans; maritime security therefore has to be a top priority in 21st century too.

India, with its geographical location and geopolitical setting in the IOR, has to play a leading role to retain its strategic position. India's interests are strategic and proximate. As one of the two largest countries in the region, and geographically located as it is, India has responsibilities in ensuring security of the commons, as well as legitimate concerns. India will have to ensure that we can safeguard our interests across this wide spread. To this menu should be added the ability to respond to natural disasters which visit the Indian Ocean region more often than they do elsewhere. A mix of capabilities, essentially maritime, is needed, ocean going as well as coastal, supported by a comprehensive and networked information, intelligence and command and control mechanisms. Ability of these systems to withstand sophisticated levels of hostile cyber warfare is equally important. To this list should be added a vibrant merchant marine served by ports that are both quantitatively and qualitatively capable of coping with the escalating need. Finally, to answer the challenges and responsibilities arising from the developing scenario, it is imperative that the nation's diplomacy and its maritime strategies function in sync with each other. A holistic approach is essential if India's sea power is first, built to the required level, and then, exploited consistent with the nation's security interests. In the long term, India aspires to maintain a strong naval presence in the entire Indian Ocean by maintaining a blue-water navy.

References

1. W. Lawrence S. Prabhakar, "Growth of Naval Power in the Indian Ocean: Dynamics and Transformation", National Maritime Foundation Monograph Series, New Delhi, 2016, p. 1.
2. Sayoni Choudhuri, "India in Indian Ocean", FPRC Journal, No. 2, New Delhi, 2013, p. 138.
3. Robert D. Kaplan, "Center Stage for the 21st Century: Power Plays in the Indian Ocean", Foreign Affairs, March/April 2009, pp. 18-19.
4. David Scott, "The Indian Ocean", in Raghavan, Malone and Mohan (eds.), Handbook of Indian Foreign Policy (Oxford: Oxford University Press, 2014).
5. See, Indian Maritime Doctrine, Indian Navy, Government of India, 2009.
6. Cited in Subhas Kapila, "India Defines Her Strategic Frontiers", South Asia Analysis Group Paper No. 832, November 4, 2003.
7. Ashok K. Behuria, "Cooperation in Indian Ocean: An Indian Perspective", Paper Presented at the Galle Dialogue, Srilanka, 14 December 2012, p. 2.
8. Admiral Arun Prakash, "Indian Maritime Doctrime", in Nambiar E.K.G. and Surya Narayan V. (eds.), Lectures on

Maritime Studies (Publications Division, University of Calicut, 2005), p. 24.

9. G S Khurana, "Maritime Security in the Indian Ocean: Convergence Plus Cooperation Equals Resonance", Strategic Analysis, Vol. 28, No. 3, July-September 2004, p. 413.

10. Sanjay Chaturvedi, "Common Security, Geopolitics, Development, South Asia and the Indian Ocean", Third World Quarterly, Vol. 19, No 4, 1998, pp. 701- 24.

11. Donald L. Berlin, "India in the Indian Ocean", Naval War College Review, Spring 2006, Vol. 59, No. 2, 2006.

12. Nirupama Rao, 'India as a Consensual Stakeholder in the Indian Ocean: Policy Contours', 19 Nov. 2010, available at *<http://www.maritimeindia.org/sites/all/files/pdf/FS_speech_ at_ NMF_Nov2010.pdf>*.

13. See, Indian Maritime Doctrine, Integrated Headquarters, Ministry of Defence, Government of India, New Delhi, 25 April 2004, p. 64.

14. Quoted in David Scott, "The Indian Ocean", in Raghavan, Malone and Mohan (eds.), Handbook of Indian Foreign Policy (Oxford: Oxford University Press, 2014).

15. M.A.H. Siddiqi, India in the Indian Ocean: A Geopolitical Study (Jaipur and New Delhi: Rawat Publications, 1997), p. 15.

16. Indian Foreign Secretary, Nirupama Rao, "India as a Consensual Stakeholder in the Indian Ocean: Policy Contours", Speech delivered at the National Maritime Foundation, India on November 19, 2010, available at*<http://www.mea.gov.in/Speeches-Statements.htm?dtl/816/Speech+by+Foreign+Secretary+at+National+Maritime+ Foundation+on+India+as+a+Consensual+Stakeholder+in+the+Indian+ Ocean+ Policy+Contours>*.

17. Sayoni Choudhuri, n. 2.

18. Prabhakaran Paleri, Role of the Coast Guard in the Maritime Security of India (New Delhi: United Service Institution of India in Association with Knowledge World, 2004), pp. 23-24.

19. Sam Bateman, "Assessing the Threat of Maritime Terrorism: Issues for the Asia-Pacific Region", Security Challenges, Vol. 2, No. 3, October 2006, p. 78.
20. Paleri Prabhakaran, n. 18, pp. 102-03.
21. Chris Rehman, "Concepts of Maritime Security: A Strategic Perspective on Alternative Visions for Good Order and Security at Sea, With Policy Implications for New Zealand", Discussion Papers, The Centre for Strategic Studies, New Zealand, 2009, p. 29, available at *<http://www.victoria.ac.nz/css/docs/Discussion_Papers/DP07-09.pdf>*.
22. Mihir Roy, "Maritime Security in South West Asia", pp. 1-2, available at *<http://www.iips.org/Roy-paper.pdf>*.
23. Address at ceremonial reception of INSV Mhadei, at Mumbai, on 06 April 2013.
24. This has been cited in P K Ghosh and Sripathy Narayan, "Maritime Capacity of India: Strength and Challenges", p.1.
25. See, Indian Maritime Doctrine, Integrated Headquarters, Ministry of Defence (Navy), Government of India, 2009.
26. Arun Prakash, "A Vision of India's Maritime Power in the 21st Century", Air Power Journal, Vol. 1 No. 2, Winter 2006, p. 4; Nirmal Kumar Verma, Address by the Chief of the Naval Staff at DSSC, Wellington', 17 March 2011, available at *<http://indiannavy.nic.in/cns-speeches/address-dssc-wellington-maritime-strategy-emerging-india>*.
27 Hari Saran and Harsh K. Sinha, "India's Maritime Stakes and Challenges in Indian Ocean", Scholar's Voice- A New Way of Thinking, Vol. 2, No. 1, Jan-June 2011, pp. 1-3.
28. Bonnor Jenelle, "Australia–India Security Relations: Common Interests or Common Disinterest?", Australian Defence Studies Centre, April 2001. 29 See, *http://www.indiannavy.nic.in/sites/default/files/Chapter1.pdf*.
30. See, Indian Maritime Doctrine, Integrated Headquarters, Ministry of Defence, Government of India, New Delhi, 25 April 2004, p. 63.

31. Admiral Arun Prakash, "Indian Maritime Doctrine", in Nambiar E.K.G. and Surya Narayan V. (eds.), Lectures on Maritime Studies, Publications Division, University of Calicut, 2005, p. 24.

32. Alok Bansal, "Synergising Indian Navy and Coast Guard", Journal of Defence Studies (New Delhi), vol. 2(1), Summer 2008, pp. 82-3.

33. David Scott, "India's 'Grand Strategy' for the Indian Ocean: Mahanian Visions", Asia-Pacific Review, Vol. 13, No. 2, 2006.

34. See, Indian Maritime Doctrine, Indian Navy, Government of India, August 2009, pp. 65-8.

35. Statement by Ambassador H.S. Puri, Permanent Representative of India on Piracy Off the Coast of Somalia at the UN Security Council on 25 January 2011, available at <http://www.un.int/india/2011/ind1815.pdf>.

36. Lecture Delivered by Vice Admiral Pradeep Chauhan on India's Maritime Interests and Navy's Transformational Role, at Observer Research Foundation, Mumbai, 21st October 2011, p. 4.

37. Hemant Krishan Singh presentation on 'Regional Security: The View From New Delhi', at the 12th India-Korea Dialogue, New Delhi, 24-25 October 2013.

38. Premvir Das, "Maritime Power: Key to India's Security Interests", Aspen Institute India, Policy Paper No. 1, Haryana, January 2011.

39. David A. Robinson, "India's Rise as a Great Power, Part One: Regional and Global Implications", in Leighton G. Luke and Tas Luttrell (eds.), Indian Ocean: A Sea of Uncertainty (West Perth, WA: Future Directions International, 2012), p. 59.

40. Sidra Tariq, "India and China in the Indian Ocean: A Complex Interplay of Geopolitics", Institute of Regional Studies, Islamabad, January-February 2014, p. 8.

41. Rupert Herbert-Burns, "Naval Power in the Indian Ocean: Evolving Roles, Missions and Capabilities", in David Michel

and Russell Sticklor (eds.), Indian Ocean Rising: Maritime Security and Policy Challenges (Washington: Stimson, July 2012), p. 49.

42. US Secretary of Defence Mr. Robert Gates Statement was quoted in Gurpreet S. Khurana, "America's Expectation versus India's Expediency: India as a Regional 'Net Security Provider'", National Maritime Foundation Issue Brief, New Delhi, 4 April 2016, p. 2.

43. Gurpreet S. Khurana, "Net Security Provider' Defined: An Analysis of India's New Maritime Strategy-2015", National Maritime Foundation, 23 November 2015.

44. Sarabjeet Singh Parmar, "Maritime Security in India Ocean: A Changing Kaleidoscope", Journal for Defence Studies, Vol. 7, No. 4, Oct-Dec, 2013.

45. Abhijit Singh, "Maritime Security Partner in the Indo-Pacific", in S D Muni and Vivek Chadha (eds.), Asian Strategic Review 2015: India as a Security Provider (New Delhi: Pentagon Press in association with Institute for Defence Studies and Analysis, 2015), pp. 149-50.

46. Cited in Ministry of Defence, 'Indian Navy's Plan "IOR" Operations Demonstrate Reach of India's Maritime Diplomacy', 13 June 2012, available at <http://pib.nic.in/newsite/erelease.aspx?relid=84863>.

4

India's Maritime Challenges: Terrorism and Piracy

The research study seeks to make a critical, descriptive analysis on the role played by maritime terrorism and piracy in influencing the maritime security in the Indian Ocean. In the 21st century, the whole concept of security has witnessed a significant transformation from a strictly land security to encompass security of the seas. Unlike the protection of the land, protection of the sea was not given much deserved priority. With growing awareness about the need to protect sea, maritime terrorism and piracy have received significant attention among the policy makers, security analysts and strategic experts with a view to tackle the issues. Maritime terrorism and piracy are increasingly posing a serious threat to the maritime security in the Indian Ocean in recent years.[1]

Political and socio-economic factors led to the renaissance of piracy as a security threat during the 1970s. However, by 1983, the problem became alarming, leading to the adoption of antipiracy measures by the international community. During the same period, maritime terrorist attacks increased, although incidents remained localised. As insurgent movements fought on land to gain independence from former colonial governments, terrorist actions spilled into the maritime domain. The attacks on the USS Cole in 2000 and on the French-registered oil tanker, Limburg, in 2002 coupled with the terrorist attacks on the United States on 11 September 2001, created fear that a captured ship could be used as a delivery platform for weapons of mass destruction (WMD) or that a ship with dangerous cargo could be used as a weapon.[2]

Pirate tends to operate in regions with large coastal areas, high levels of commercial activity, small national naval forces and weak regional security cooperation mechanisms. Piracy off the coast of Somalia in the Gulf of Aden in the Indian Ocean region has become a significant non-traditional security challenge to many nations. The increasing number of such attacks as a result of failure of Somali government to tackle its internal problem drew the attention of international community who lent a drastic response thereby curtailing the number of such incidents significantly now.[3] Initially, pirate activities occur at a very low level, mainly concentrated in the Gulf of Aden. Later, the scope of pirate activities expanded to include a much higher frequency of attacks carried out off Somalia's Indian Ocean coast by larger and more organized pirate groups. However, since 2007, Somali pirates have again - and even more dramatically - increased both the number and range of their attacks. Although the number of successful attacks carried has declined since 2011, Somali pirates are still capable of hijacking large merchant vessels hundreds of miles offshore.[4] India in particular is seriously concerned about the protection of sea against the threats posed by maritime terrorism and piracy. India, being the most important economic player and economic giant among the countries in Asia, engages in a large volume of maritime trade with major global and regional powers in the world. It is the thirteenth largest importer in the world with approximately 90 per-cent of its total trade by volume, and 70 per cent by value, transported by sea. Trade accounts for around 51 per cent of its GDP, of which approximately 52 per cent is handled by major ports on the western coast. Furthermore, an estimated US$ 110 billion worth in Indian trade transits through the Gulf of Aden each year. Besides, India imports 75 per cent of its oil supply from the Middle East.[5]

If maritime terrorism has largely remained a virtual threat, the breakthrough for maritime security came with the rise of piracy off the coast of Somalia between 2008 and 2011. The dangers of piracy for international trade brought the maritime dimension of security to the global consciousness and lifted it high on policy agendas. The chapter is organised in this manner – first, it makes a conceptual analysis of the maritime terrorism and piracy by defining it from the contemporary perspective. It then highlights the similarities and differences between maritime terrorism and piracy. Secondly, it discusses the maritime security challenges in the Indian Ocean in general and in particular to maritime terrorism threats and piracy threats in the Indian Ocean. Besides, it explains on how to address the emerging challenges posed by the threats of maritime terrorism and threats. Further, it highlights India's anti-piracy operations in the Indian Ocean.

Conceptualising Maritime Terrorism and Piracy

Conceptualising maritime terrorism and piracy is never an easy task when there is no such universally accepted definition on both the concept. Perceptions of the threat of terrorism both at sea and by illegal use of the maritime transportation system have led to dramatic changes in maritime security arrangements in recent years. It is important though to ensure lack of knowledge and awareness does not lead to over-reaction. A careful balance is required between tighter security and the efficient flow of trade. This balance can be disturbed by the introduction of measures to ensure greater maritime security at a national level, which fail to take full account of the implications of such measures for international maritime industry more generally.

In order to distinguish between piracy, acts of armed robbery of ships and maritime terrorism it is necessary to define these concepts and identify the origins of these definitions.

Defining Maritime Terrorism

Before going directly into defining maritime terrorism, it would be necessary to define the terrorism first. Ranstorp and Wilkinson has defined terrorism as, '... the systematic use of coercive intimidation usually, though not exclusively, to service political ends. It is used to create and exploit a climate of fear among a wider group than the immediate victims of the violence, often to publicise a cause, as well as to coerce a target into acceding to terrorist aims.[6]

There is no universally accepted definition of maritime terrorism. Maritime terrorism is defined as:

- Any attempt or threat to seize control of a ship by force;
- To damage or destroy a ship or its cargo;
- To injure or kill a person on board a ship; or
- To endanger in any way the safe navigation of a ship that moves from the territorial waters of one State into those of another State or into international waters.[7]

The Council for Security Cooperation in the Asia Pacific (CSCAP) Working Group has offered an extensive definition for maritime terrorism: "...the undertaking of terrorist acts and activities within the maritime environment, using or against vessels or fixed platforms at sea or in port, or against any one of their passengers or personnel, against coastal facilities or settlements, including tourist resorts, port areas and port towns or cities."[8] In other words, maritime terrorism may be defined as 'terrorist attacks executed within, or with the intent of compromising the features of the maritime domain.'[9] Maritime terrorism includes attack of threat of attacks against vessels (warships, cruise liners, tankers and other carriers, tugboats and barges), harbour attacks, fixed land based targets near ports – oil refineries, oil storage depots, other ports infrastructure, energy pipelines – and hijacking of commercial / passenger ships on high seas. Maritime terrorism, therefore, as the use or threat of violence against a ship (civilian as well as military), its passengers or sailors, cargo, a port facility, or if the purpose is solely a platform for political ends. The definition can be expanded to include the use of the maritime transportation system to smuggle terrorists or terrorist materials into the targeted country. Maritime terrorism is motivated by political goals beyond the immediate act of attacking a maritime target. Terrorist can develop effective attack capabilities relatively quickly using a variety of platforms including–

- Explosives laden suicide boats and light aircraft;
- Merchant and cruise ships as kinetic weapons to ram another vessel, warship, port facility, or offshore platform;
- Commercial vessels as launch platforms for missile attacks;
- Underwater swimmer to infiltrate ports; and
- Unmanned underwater explosive delivery vehicle.[10]

Martin Murphy highlighted eight factors which are being considered as favourable conditions for maritime terrorism: legal and jurisdictional opportunities; geographical necessity; inadequate security; secure base areas; maritime tradition; charismatic and effective leadership; state support; and promise of reward.[11] Maritime terrorism, like all forms of terrorism, has mostly a political, ideological or religious background. Terrorists will therefore ask themselves where they can hit the infrastructure of the industrialized world most effectively. They may focus their attention on so called choke points and mega-harbours, with 75 per- cent of all international sea transport activities carried out by around 50,000 ships using 2,800 ports. The strategically important Strait of Malacca is one of the critical choke points. It connects the Indian Ocean with the South China Sea and the Pacific. It is the most significant trade route between the Far East, the Gulf States and Europe. 90,000 ships use the Strait every year and one third of the world trade, 80 per cent of oil exports to East Asia and two thirds of LNG exports pass through the Strait of Malacca.[12]

Defining Piracy

Both the United Nations (UN)'s International Maritime Organization (IMO) and the International Maritime Bureau (IMB) currently use the definition of piracy as described in the United Nations Convention on the Law of the Sea (UNCLOS). In article 101 of the 1982 United Nations Convention on the Law of the Sea (UNCLOS), Piracy is defined as follows:

a. any illegal acts of violence or detention, or any act of depredation, committed for private ends by the crew or the passengers of a private ship or a private aircraft, and directed:

   - on the high seas, against another ship or aircraft, or against persons or property on board such ship or aircraft;
   - against a ship, aircraft, persons or property in a place outside the jurisdiction of any State;

b. any act of voluntary participation in the operation of a ship or of an aircraft with knowledge of facts making it a pirate ship or aircraft;

c. any act of inciting or of intentionally facilitating an act described in subparagraph a or b.[13]

According to this definition, piracy is limited to acts outside the jurisdiction of the coastal waters of a state. Acts committed in coastal waters are considered armed robbery. This means that many cases of violence against ships occurring in the territorial waters of states are excluded from this definition. This also excludes acts of maritime terrorism, as political objectives are not included in this definition.[14]

The International Maritime Organization (IMO) in its 26th Assembly session defines Armed Robbery in Resolution A.1025 "Code of Practice for the Investigation of Crimes of Piracy and Armed Robbery against Ships" as follows: "Armed robbery against ships," means any of the following acts:

- any unlawful act of violence or detention or any act of depredation, or threat thereof, other than an act of piracy, committed for private ends and directed against a ship or against a person or property on board such a ship, within a State's internal waters, archipelagic waters and territorial sea;
- any act of inciting or of intentionally facilitating an act described above.[15]

In order to overcome the distinctions between high seas and territorial waters, the International Maritime Bureau (IMB, 2009) in its annual report, defined piracy as,

> 'an act of boarding or attempting to board any ship with the apparent intent to commit theft or any other crime and with the apparent intent or capability to use force in the furtherance of that act'.

Issues arising from the definition of IMB above, is that, intent, specification, extent and the use of force are principal elements to be considered in what constitute piracy and not necessarily where or location of occurrence.[16] Established by the International Chamber of Commerce (ICC) in 1981, the International Maritime Bureau (IMB) came into existence with the backing of the IMO, the world's foremost agency for exchanging and collecting information on maritime crime. However, according to the IMO, it is estimated that piracy incidents are likely under-reported by a factor of two (meaning, they assume that for each attack that was announced, there were two additional attacks that were not announced). Moreover, it is likely that the statistics are subject to distortion as many smaller attacks go unreported. This mainly stems from two factors:

1. the increase in insurance premiums often outweigh the value of the claim for smaller attacks; and
2. Reporting a piracy attack is often time-consuming can lead to a delay of several days. Keeping in mind the running sunk costs of an idle ship (up to $25,000 per day), in many, especially smaller cases, it is cheaper not to report the incident.[17]

Martin N. Murphy has in his book, '*Small boats, weak states and dirty money*' defines piracy as "unlawful depredation at sea involving the use or threat of violence possibly, but not necessarily, involving robbery... Piracy, while not a political crime, has invariably been linked to politics and the expression of state power, or more commonly weakness..."[18] Maritime piracy is a maritime transport issue that directly affects ships, ports, terminals, cargo and seafarers. Above all, piracy is associated with considerable human costs, as seafarers are the first to be affected by piracy attacks. They are usually held hostageand may be injured or killed. There are different forms of piracy ranging - maritime and coastal piracy, capers and corsairs. The piracy occurs on the high seas where no state is sovereign. Piracy is indiscriminate, meaning that any vessel originating from any state is fair game. The fact that piracy occurs in an ungoverned space and has the potential to impact all states has made piracy a problem "of the commons" requiring a collective solution.[19]

Piracy consists of the following main forms of

criminal activity:

- Harbor and anchorage attacks
- Attacks against vessels at sea—(sea) robbery, sometimes also referred to as "Asian piracy"
- Attacks against vessels at sea—hijacking accompanied by the neutralization of the crew (a variation of this can include the permanent seizure of a vessel by pirates)
- Kidnap for ransom[20]

Differences and Similarities between Piracy and Maritime Terrorism

From the above definition of both the concept of maritime terrorism and piracy, it can be observed that maritime terrorism is only one of the areas of operation for terrorist organisations. John Patch, a renowned scholar in the areas of maritime security states that, "The distinction between piracy and terrorism is neither semantic nor academic. If for piracy, the responsibility lies with local law enforcement officials, not the military. But maritime terrorism means scrambling the Navy."[21]

It is being said that terrorists have developed some capabilities to either adopt pirates' tactics or "piggyback" on pirates' raid. It is also viewed that maritime terrorists, rather than simply stealing, could either blow up the ship or use it to ram into another vessel or a port facility. Terrorist groups even regard seaports and international cruise liners as very attractive terrorist targets because they reside in the nexus of terrorist intent, capability, and opportunity.[22] The possible links between maritime pirates and terrorists are also limited, as the objectives of these organisations differ. Pirates have financial motives, while terrorists have political motives. Probably the best distinction between pirates and terrorists is their motives. The pirates are influenced by the financial benefits, whereas, the terrorists are influenced by political factors. Although cooperation between these groups is unlikely, it is not impossible and could be dangerous especially in vulnerable areas such as the coast of Somalia, the Red Sea and the Gulf of Aden. The key causes of piracy includes geography, weak law enforcement, maritime insecurity, economic dislocation, cultural acceptability and the prevalence of criminal entrepreneurs.[23]

Another distinction is the use of violence. In most cases, pirates try to prevent loss of life for fear of retaliation by foreign navies. Currently, foreign navies in Somalia do not interfere with ships once they have been pirated because of the risk piracy holds to human life. The opposite is true for terrorists where publicity usually increases with greater loss of human life. Pirates make use of simple tactics, while terrorists use more sophisticated tactics. Piracy also takes place at local or regional level, while terrorists can have a more global reach in terms of objectives. There are, however, terrorist groups that operate only at local or regional level and aim to fulfil political agendas at local level.[24] Pirates would also normally try to avoid attention, while terrorists seek attention to promote their cause.

From the point of view of similarities, both pirates and maritime terrorists operate in the maritime environment using ships or boats and must have the skills to operate such vessels. In both cases, actions are mostly aimed at civilians and have a human cost attached to operations, and both groups can operate across borders.[25] Small, fast boats are often chosen for operations for their speed, manoeuvrability, effectiveness to evade radar detection and because they are less expensive to acquire and maintain than large vessels. Both groups also need a land base from which to operate. Pirates and maritime terrorists both become more effective as they get more organised and both make use of intelligence to plan actions. Violence or the threat of violence is also utilised by both groups. Pirates as well as terrorist organisations need funds to sustain their operations.[26] Both pirates and terrorists will also have an effect on the socio-economic and political security in the areas where they operate.[27]

Table 4.1

Piracy, Armed Robbery against Ships, Maritime terrorism

	Piracy	**Armed Robbery against Ships**	**Maritime Terrorism**
Authoritative Source	The 1982 United Nations Conventions on the law of the sea, Article 101.	The IMO decision – Code of Practice for the investigation of Crimes of Piracy and Armed Robbery against ships.	Absent of authoritative definitions; The one elaborated by the Council for security Cooperation in the Asia Pacific (CSCAP) Working group is much referred to.
Characteristics	- For private ends; - Against another ship; - on the high seas.	- For private ends; - Against another ship; - Within a state's internal waters, archipelagic waters and territorial sea.	- Forms of terrorist acts and activities; - Within the marine environment.
Legal Status	Codified international law	With weighing referential values	A working definition by CSCAP

Source: Hui-Yi Katherine Tseng, "Maritime Security in Southeast Asia: Interfacing Regional and Extra-Regional Stakeholder", in *Maritime Security and Piracy: Common Challenges and Responses from Europe and Asia* (Singapore: Konrad-Adenauer Stiftung and European Union, 2014), p. 91

Maritime Security Challenges in the Indian Ocean

Maritime Security challenges in the Indian Ocean have many faces – piracy and armed robbery, maritime terrorism, illicit trafficking by sea, i.e. narcotics trafficking, small arms and light weapons trafficking, human trafficking, global climate change, cargo theft, etc. These challenges keep evolving and may be hybrid in nature: an interconnected and unpredictable mix of traditional and irregular warfare, terrorism, and/or organized crime.

Maritime threats are inter-connected. Different threats, such as trafficking, piracy and terrorism potentially re-enforce each other since they thrive in insecure waters in which violence is common and the law is not adequately enforced. In recent years, maritime piracy has received the majority of attention. Indeed, the maritime security agenda, especially in the Western Indian Ocean, has been dominated by the issue, and most resources have been devoted to curbing it.[28]

The smuggling of people, drugs, weapons, and other contraband, as well as piracy and armed robbery against vessels, pose a threat to maritime security. Piracy and incidents of maritime crime tend to be concentrated in areas of heavy commercial maritime activity, especially where there is significant political and economic instability, or in regions with little or no maritime law enforcement capacity. Today's pirates and criminals are usually well organized and well equipped with advanced communications, weapons, and high speed craft. The capabilities to board and commandeer large underway vessels demonstrated in numerous piracy incidents - could also be employed to facilitate terrorist acts.[29]

Modern piracy is a complex problem that is often the manifestation of various underlying socio-political problems. Hence, piracy emanating from an area is often unique in its approach and distinct from piracy incidents in other regions of the world. The solution to eradicating this scourge does not exclusively lie at sea and requires a multi-pronged approach to tackle the root of the problem rather than focus on an exclusive naval usage to merely suppress it.

Maritime Terrorism and Piracy: Threats to Indian Ocean

With increasing maritime trade, the activities of piracy and maritime terrorism pose a serious threat to the world's Oceans and in particular to the Indian Ocean. Maritime terrorism and piracy have been great threats to the security of the international waters for a long time. Previous incidents have demonstrated that determined maritime terrorists could cause serious damage in any sea borne vessel let it be a defenceless commercial oil tanker or a heavily armoured military cruiser. A well-planned and precisely executed act of sea borne terrorism in any of the strategically important maritime straits, canals or ports could easily bring the regional and global economy to a halt to an extent when specific countries might remain without energy sources for a short period of time. The international community is well aware of the fact that terrorism and piracy at sea pose a threat to any potential target. In order for policymakers to develop and implement the most effective counterstrategy, they must first understand their nature and the conditions that give rise to them.

Piracy and maritime terrorism have become the "new" threats to maritime security in the Asia-Pacific region. While acts of piracy and armed robbery against ships have a long history in Asian waters, particularly in Southeast Asia, international interest in the piracy threat has been much higher in recent years. Several factors explain this. First, the incidence of piracy and armed robbery against ships has led to assessments of higher risks of terrorist attack, and actions to counter piracy are seen as also reducing the risks of terrorist attack.[30]

The vast and largely ungoverned maritime domain is an area that terrorists and pirates actively seek to exploit in pursuit of achieving their land-based goals and objectives. Piracy is a dangerous threat to international maritime trade, especially in the area off the Somalian coast, the southern Red Sea, the Gulf of Aden as well as the Arabian Sea. Eighty per cent of the world's cargo is carried by sea on more than 112000 ships manned by more than 1.5 million seafarers, and as the maritime domain is an unregulated area, ships and crew on these ships are vulnerable to maritime violence. Thousands of ports and harbour facilities serviced by hundreds of thousands of port staff are also vulnerable to maritime criminals and terrorists. Attacks by terrorists, pirates and criminals operating in the maritime environment also have the potential to affect global trade.[31]

Among the world's Oceans, Indian Ocean is considered as a more "active" ocean as it is hosting a spectrum of activities ranging from extensive trade, transportation to important energy transfers which are quantitative as well as qualitatively much larger in scope and size. Given that nearly 100,000 ships transit the expanse of the Indian Ocean annually, it is a very trade busy ocean. It is perhaps the only ocean through which SLOCs (Sea Lines of Communication) reach out to the entire world, be it those originating from the Persian Gulf with oil and gas laden ships, or those with other cargo or commodities from the littorals as well as transiting ships from the Far East. Significantly, some of the world's most important choke points and narrow passages provide access to the Indian Ocean, and these can have associated vulnerabilities.[32]

The maritime terrorism is seen as a combinational of illegal actions that affect directly or indirectly, the interests of a national at sea or on land. Terrorist and pirates possess faster boats, more fire power and safer communications than many of the governments in the region. Their attacks become more intensive and effective, often causing higher number of casualties. These attacks affect negatively navies, coast guard organisations, navigation and whole societies. Among the targets of terrorist and pirate attacks are vessels, port facilities and equipment. Damaged caused by maritime terrorism to the international market of cargo shipping are estimated in the billions of dollars not including fear and other psychological effects on the citizens.[33]

Maritime Terrorism during the Period between 1945 and 1990

Incidents of maritime terrorism were high in the second half of the 20th century. Between 1979 and 1989, 47 terrorist attacks on ships were reported.[34] During these incidents, eight vessels were hijacked and 11 ships were destroyed. Although the hijacking of the Santa Maria in 1961 was the first such case of maritime terrorism in the 20th century. While, the Achille Lauro incident in 1985 created far-reaching publicity and influenced international relations. The hijacking of Italian passenger ship was carried out by the battle group of terrorist organisation named 'Front for Liberation of Palestine' in the eastern Mediterranean. The Santa Maria hijacking in 1961 is regarded as the first incident of modern maritime terrorism. The hijacking internationalised conditions in Portugal's colonies in Africa and as a result, Angola was placed on the UN Security Council's agenda in 1961. The hijacking also sparked the 1961 uprising in Angola.[35]

The Palestinians were involved in maritime terrorism in the role of attackers (six cases between 1971 and 1985) as well as victims, usually involving Israeli or rival forces.[36] One of these incidents was the hijacking of the Achille Lauro. On 7 October 1985, the cruise liner Achille Lauro, with more than 750 passengers and 331 crew members on board, made a stop at Alexandra, where 651 of the passengers disembarked, planning to meet the ship again in Port Said.[37]

Maritime Terrorism Post 1991

Although, there exists, no such exclusively maritime terrorist organisations. Prior to 2000, incidents of maritime terrorism were higher, especially in the second half of the 20th century, compared to maritime terrorist incidents between 2000 and 2016. Only a few actual proven cases of maritime terrorism occurred in the last 30 years (two per cent of all global incidents in the last 30 years were seaborne terrorist strikes).[38] Even though few maritime terrorism attacks occurred after 2000, the 9/11 incident underlined the potential danger of such attacks. In January 2000, Al Qaeda's affiliate, the Aden Abyan Islamic Army (AAIA), implemented a new strategy to attack high-profile US targets including maritime targets. Boats loaded with explosives could be remotely detonated or used as suicide weapons by ramming other vessels. Such an attack on the USS Sullivan in January 2000 failed when the suicide boat, overloaded with explosives, sank in the Port of Aden.[39]

The attacks on the USS Cole in 2000, the Limburg in 2002 and the 9/11 attack in the US in 2001 created fear of a potential catastrophic terrorist attack in the maritime domain. As a result of these attacks and an all-time high in incidents of maritime piracy and armed robbery of ships in 2000, maritime piracy and terrorism were increasingly linked and became highly controversial subjects. In October 2002, the French-registered oil tanker, Limburg, carrying crude oil off the coast of Yemen was bombed using a small boat loaded with explosives. Ninety thousand barrels of oil spilled into the Gulf of Aden leading to huge financial losses for Yemen in the form of tourist cancellations, cost of cleaning-up operations and consequent limited use of the port.[40]

In 2004, the Abu Sayyaf Group (ASG) bombed Philippine Superferry 14 carrying 899 passengers[41] by placing a bomb in a television set, killing more than a hundred people. The ferry company, Sulpicio and William, Gothong and Aboitiz (WG&A) lines, received an extortion letter prior to the bombing, demanding one million dollars for the safe use of the waters of Mindanao.[42]

Attacks at sea are not simple operations and hold their own difficulties. Concealment during surveillance at sea offers more problems than on land. Attacks on some maritime terrorist targets could potentially be very damaging to human life and the environment and could lead to high financial losses. Such potential targets are "chokepoints", global container trans-shipment hub ports, world oil supply lines, cruise ships and passenger ferries. 'Chokepoints' are narrow straits through which vessels are forced to travel, such as the Malacca and Singapore Straits and the Suez Canal. The closure of a hub port housing container trans-shipment facilities such as Singapore, Hong Kong and Rotterdam could lead to the loss of millions of dollars a day and an attack on such a port could lead to high losses in terms of human life.[43] A maritime terrorist attack mounted at a natural choke point would provide a significant strategic advantage while also increasing collateral damage. For example, the Bab-el-Mandeb Strait is only 30 km wide. Everyday large oil tankers transit this narrow strait carrying over 3.4 million barrels of crude oil and are unable to manoeuvre freely, increase speed or avoid visual detection by heading farther offshore.[44] The fear exists that terrorists could deliver a nuclear, chemical, biological or radiological device, weapon or substance to a target destination through the use of cargo containers. Explosives on a ship or smaller boat could also be remotely detonated or used as a suicide weapon by ramming another vessel.

Piracy Threats

Several socio-economic and political factors contribute to maritime piracy and acts of armed robbery of ships, such as underdevelopment and political instability, criminality and corruption, and ineffective government and law enforcement agencies.[45] Small and inadequate navies and coast guards also contribute to the existence of piracy and armed robbery of ships, especially if there is a lack of will to act on reported incidents.[46] The Somalia piracy has a deep rooted financial and security implications, reflecting the need for urgent actions among the maritime countries of the world including India. The high cost of piracy has undoubtedly spurred cooperation. The total cost of piracy off the Horn of Africa, including public and private counter-piracy efforts, is estimated to be around US$ 7–12 billion annually.[47] Piracy has a direct economic impact in terms of fraud, stolen cargos and delayed trips.[48] Besides, it also affects all the shipping companies placing 'extra insurance costs' on them. It is evidently estimated that the payment of ransom to pirates have raised substantially the costs of claims.[49]

As piracy activities have evolved and become more widespread and complex, the issue of maritime piracy has developed into a multifaceted transnational security challenge that threatens lives, livelihoods and global welfare. Piracy gives rise to considerable direct and second order costs and has broad repercussions both at a regional and at a global level. Piracy disrupts transport and trade flows as well as other economic activities, such as fisheries and energy production, thus potentially jeopardizing the development prospects of both coastal and landlocked economies in affected regions. Moreover, piracy threatens the safety of navigation and delivery of humanitarian aid and has broader implications for transport and trade across interconnected global supply chains, as well as for energy and food security.

The Somalia piracy is focused on the hijacking of ships and the securing of ransom for their release. An example typical of this type of pirate attack involved the Bahamian-ûagged MV CEC Future, which was hijacked in November 2008. The pirates were armed with AK-47s, a rocket-propelled grenade launcher, and handguns when they attacked and seized the vessel, which was owned by Clipper Group, a Danish company. The pirates forced the crew to anchor off the Somalia coast and held the vessel, cargo, and 13 crew members captive for 71 days until the owners delivered $1.7 million in ransom to the pirates. One of the two leaders of the pirate group was shot dead in a battle over the ransom as soon as he arrived ashore.[50]

Table 4.2

Piracy Attacks Worldwide

Year	Strait of Malacca	South China Sea	Indian Ocean	East Asia	West Asia	South America	Mediterranean
1998	6	94	25	19	22	38	2
2000	112	140	109	29	33	41	2
2002	34	140	66	23	47	67	3
2004	60	113	41	13	57	46	0
2006	20	97	51	49	23	26	0
2008	2	23	-	63	24	-	-
2009*	8	10	22	100	-	28	-

* The Figure in 2009 is available till September.

Source: Annushree Bhattacharyya Chakarborty, "Coping the Piracy Menace in the Gulf of Aden: Security Imperatives, *Asia Pacific Journal of Social Sciences,* Vol. 1, No. 2, July-December 2009, p. 74.

Between 2000 and end of May 2013, a total of 4 759 incidents of piracy and acts of armed robbery of ships occurred worldwide. Although there was a sharp increase in incidents (attempted and actual attacks) in Somalia in 2009, the number of successful hijackings of ships remained constant and attacks were proportionally less successful, which could be attributed to the presence of a foreign navy in these waters. In 2010, a ten per cent increase in piracy-related incidents was reported, which was mainly due to an increase in pirate activity in Indonesian waters.[51] Attacks by Somalian pirates remained constant, but their success rate increased with 49 ships hijacked and 1016 crew members taken hostage. This indicated that pirates adapted to the higher foreign naval presence by expanding their area of operation more than 1000 NM from the Somali coast into the Eastern Red Sea, Oman in the Arabian Sea and the Indian Ocean as far as the Maldives.[52]

In 2011, Somalia pirates launched 176 attacks during which 25 ships were pirated.[53] A total of 75 attacks were attributed to Somalia pirates in 2012, during which 14 hijackings took place and 250 hostages were taken. Attacks were lower in 2012 due to the presence of security teams on board ships, increased ship's hardening, the efforts of naval forces in the area and land-based anti-piracy operations.[54]

Maritime piracy and acts of armed robbery of ships range between opportunity theft when a ship is at berth, hit-and-run attacks mostly at night where pirates or maritime criminals rob a ship or crew, and attacks with the intent to take the crew hostage (worldwide 5956 crew members were taken hostage between 2003[55] and 2012[56]) or to hijack the ship for ransom or mother ship services. The levels of violence and financial losses due to attacks differ according to the type of attack but also according to the geographical location where the attack occurs. Almost all attacks in Somalia, the Red Sea and the Gulf of Aden took place while vessels were cruising, and hijacking was the motive in almost all the cases.[57] Pirate attacks in Somalia range from unplanned attacks to well-organised attacks with the intention to hijack the ship and to hold both ship and crew for ransom.[58] Automatic weapons and rocket-propelled grenade launchers (RPGs) are used during attacks.

Increase of piracy in Somalia waters has been a threat to international shipping and commercial seaborne trade. At present about 95 per cent of the piracy in international waters is done by Somali pirates. The area has now overtaken the Straits of Malacca in Southeast Asia Moreover it has become an organized industry with pirates acquiring new levels of confidence where they are trying to negotiate prisoner exchange. A recent incident is a case in point where the pirates decided to retain seven Indian sailors as hostages after releasing the ship and receiving the full ransom from its Mumbai-based owner, in order to negotiate the release of 120 Somali pirates held in Indian jails. Analysts say that this new assertiveness on the part of pirates could be a result of the encouragement they get from terrorist groups.

There are fears that the ungoverned territories of Somalia could become a terrorist state financed by pirate revenues. This further raises concerns about the security of the Indian Ocean region.

Figure 4.1

Piracy Attacks: 2008-2011

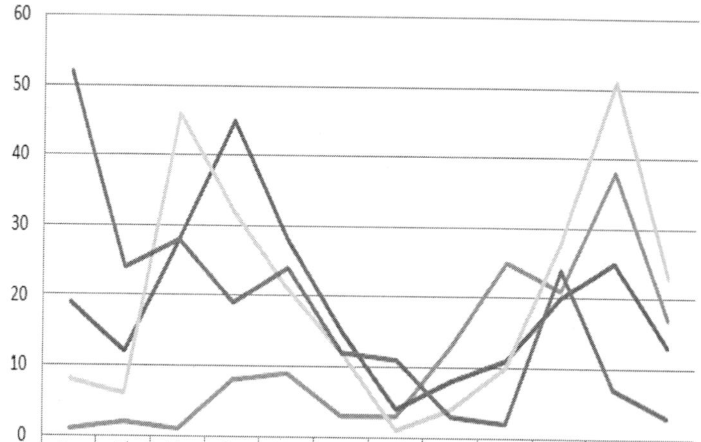

	Jan	Feb	Mar	Apr	May	Jun	Jul	Aug	Sep	Oct	Nov	Dec
2008	1	2	1	8	9	3	3	13	25	21	38	17
2009	19	12	28	45	28	15	4	8	11	20	25	13
2010	8	6	46	32	21	12	1	4	10	28	51	23
2011	52	24	28	19	24	12	11	3	2	24	7	3

Source: Rupert Herbert-Burns, "Countering Piracy, Trafficking, and Terrorism: Ensuring Maritime Security in the Indian Ocean", in David Michel and Russell Sticklor (eds.), *Indian Ocean Rising: Maritime Security and Policy Challenges* (Washington: Stimson, July 2012), p. 25.

According to the information released by Ministry of Shipping, 495 Indian seafarers were held hostages by the Somali pirates since 2007. Of them, 200 were taken captive on board foreign flag ships and 295 from about 20 Indian Motor Support Vehicles (MSVs). Barring 64, the rest of 495 hostages were released safely by March 2011. The 64 seafarers to be rescued were crew members of 6 ships: MV

Iceberg, MV Rak Afrikana, MV Suez, MV Asphalt Venture, MV Savina Caylyn, and MV Sinin that were highjacked in 2010-2011. Two of the foreign flag ships MV Savina Caylyn, and MV Sinin, with 26 Indian hostages were hijacked in January and February 2011.

On 27th of June 2011, Defence Minister A.K. Antony said - Unless a united and a combined effort under the United Nations takes place, I do not think it will be easy to defeat this threat of piracy, Defence Minister A.K. Antony told reporters in responding to questions on the increased incidence of Somali pirates taking Indian sea –farers as hostages for ransom and/ or bargain the release of Somali pirates in Indian custody. When the international forces are pushing them away from the Gulf of Aden, they are pushing too far he said referring to the ongoing anti-piracy operations in the Gulf of Aden by navies of almost all the important countries in the world, including India.[59]

Addressing Maritime Terrorism and Piracy

Addressing the threat of maritime terrorism, excellent intelligence is a necessity. The groups of greatest concern in the Gulf of Aden, the Red Sea, off the coast of Somalia are Al-Qaeda in the Arabian Peninsula (AQAP), the Abdullah Azzam Brigades and to a reduced extent Al-Shabaab.[60] To combat maritime terrorism the Container Security Initiative (CSI), initiated by the United States in 2002, is very helpful. The aim of this program is to identify – out of the 230 million containers transported by sea every year – those containers with weapons of mass destruction or dangerous nuclear substances, which could be used by terrorists for their attacks.

Counter-piracy may be organized in three layers – The first layer is that of a practitioner layer in which operational staff could engage with each other on an everyday basis free from larger political considerations (as provided for instance by the Mercury system or the Maritime Security Centre

Horn of Africa, MSCHoA). The second layer is a tactical layer in which practitioners could set tactical objectives and agree on basic operational measures (as provided by the Shared Awareness and Deconfliction Mechanism, SHADE). The third layer is a political-strategic layer in which larger strategic narratives could be aligned, mid-term objectives identified and networking opportunities between different actors established (as provided by the plenary of the CGPCS and its working group one). In this organizational design, notably the first layer can drive many pragmatic solutions forward and time is not lost in developing grand strategy with little resemblance to actual operational needs.[61]

The rise in transnational threats in the Indian Ocean region has also led to the adoption of enhanced cooperative approaches between navies of various Indian ocean littoral countries in the form of numerous anti-piracy patrols which operate in the area that have resulted in the eventual decrease in the number of piracy attacks. But the challenge remains as attacks continue to take place in further ranges due to the usage of sophisticated technologies by pirates and other non-state actors.

Increased attention to the piracy problem has led to the deployment of three types of multinational naval operations seeking to control Somali piracy: (1) a NATO-led force (Operation Ocean Shield); (2) an EU force (EUNAVFOR's Operation Atlanta); and (3) a multinational force comprising 24 nations, including the United States (CTF-151). Such a counter-piracy network has specifically aimed to reduce pirate attacks in the Indian Ocean. Piracy off the Horn of Africa rose sharply after 2008, with the number of attacks increasing from 24 in that year to 163 in 2009, reaching a high of 172 in 2011. In 2012, the number of attacks fell to 35, and in 2013, there were only 7. Of the 2013 attacks, none resulted in taking a vessel hostage. In 2014, there were two attacks, neither of which was successful; and in 2015, no attacks took place. This remarkable decline suggests that international naval missions in the Indian Ocean have been effective.[62]

India's Counter-Piracy Operations

India has a strong interest in ensuring the security of maritime traffic as piracy incurs a tremendous cost on India's maritime trade and threatens its prospects as a trading superpower. India's trade that passes through the Gulf of Aden estimated at about 110 billion dollars annually. And about 24 Indian flagged merchant ships transit the Gulf of Aden every month.

The responses to deal with the threat of piracy in Somalia waters so far have been military and police action. India on its part has been maintaining a naval presence since 2008 in the piracy prone areas in the Gulf of Aden and has been rendering assistance to merchant ships irrespective of the nationality. India's Permanent Representative the United Nations Ambassador Hardeep Singh Puri on 25 January 2011 said - Since October 2008, when it commenced anti-piracy patrols there, the Indian navy has deployed 23 ships in the Gulf of Aden and escorted to safety 1487 ships, including 1321 foreign flagged vessels from different countries, - India's Permanent Representative the United Nations, Ambassador Hardeep Singh Puri informed the Security Council on 25 January 2011. Indian naval patrol thwarted 26 piracy attempts and no ships under Indian escort were hijacked. India has a 24x7 Communication Centre to coordinate and facilitate prompt anti-piracy action. It has banned operation of Indian Dhows in piracy infested areas and made additional deployments off Eastern and North Eastern Arabian Sea to check the piracy movement west ward. Indian Navy is on patrol in the EEZ of Seychelles and Mauritius and its ships and aircrafts routinely visit waters off the Maldives.[63] Further, Ambassador Puri expressed India's support for the comprehensive report and proposed a 5 point agenda of action:

a. Reinforcement of tracking the trail of ransom money as was entrusted to the Interpol in the 6th CGPOS;
b. Prosecution of the beneficiaries of ransom money for abetting piracy;
c. Consideration of the conduct of the naval operations under the UN as the preferred option;
d. Sanitization of the Somali coast line through identified corridors and buffer zones and tracking of fishing vessels around the Somali coast;
e. Enactment of national laws on priority to criminalize piracy as defined in the UNCLOS prosecution of suspected, and imprisonment of convicted, pirates as required under Resolution 1918 (2010).

The Indian Coast Guard (ICG) the primary agency responsible for Maritime-Search and Rescue (M-SAR) in the region views the maritime security situation off the Somali coast as a continuing challenge for safe and secure maritime commercial activities. In introducing its 2011 Bi-annual Report, Chairman of National M-SAR Board, Vice Admiral Anil Chopra takes serious note of the recent spurt in incidents of hijacking of Indian sailing vessels (Dhows). The M-SAR report makes extensive references to the 'Djibouti Code of Conduct' (DCOC) in countering acts of piracy against ships in the Gulf of Aden, the Red Sea and the Western Indian Ocean. It cites the International Maritime Organization (IMO) established ad hoc trust fund (The IMO DCOC Trust Fund), to support the IMO directed technical cooperation and capacity building programmes for repression of piracy and armed robbery against ships off the coast of Somalia. The Indian Navy and the ICG have placed their ships on anti-piracy vigil around the Lakshadweep Islands due to heightened pirate activity in the Arabian Sea since November 2010. The ICG has opened a new district headquarters in Kavatti and a station in Minicoy in the

Lakshadweep Islands in December last. The Indian Coast Guard demanded jetties for its ships at Jawaharlal Nehru Port Trust in Mumbai and asked for land to set up bases in the Thane and Raigad districts. The Maharashtra government recently allotted its airport at Ratnagiri to the Coast Guard. The latest request was made to the Maharashtra Home Minister, R R Patil and Opposition leaders Eknath Khadse and Pandurang Phundkar by the Coast Guard after taking them all for a visit into the Arabian Sea off Mumbai on India's west coast that is closest to the recent piracy assaults farthest from the Somali east coast. The Coast Guard wants the state government police - to improve the flow of intelligence exchange with them, and not have interactions only at the time of joint exercises.[64]

Also to combat piracy, India uses its UAVs (Unmanned Aerial Vehicles). There are two main types of UAVs: drones and remotely piloted vehicles. To our knowledge, the major suppliers of UAVs for counter-piracy missions are the US, India and Spain. Since India's UAVs are deployed for various national security activities in the region, Third of those UAVs were used towards counter-piracy activities.

Table 4.3

India's UAVs to Combat Somali Piracy (2011)

UAVs Model	No. of Unit	Units Cost	Missions per Day	Mission Duration (Hours)	Counter Piracy Initiatives
Searcher II	100	$7,500,000	50	14	33 %
Heron	50	$10,000,000	25	24	33 %

Source: State of Maritime Piracy (OBP) Report, 2011, p. 27.

Map 4.1

India's Maritime Search and Rescue Region

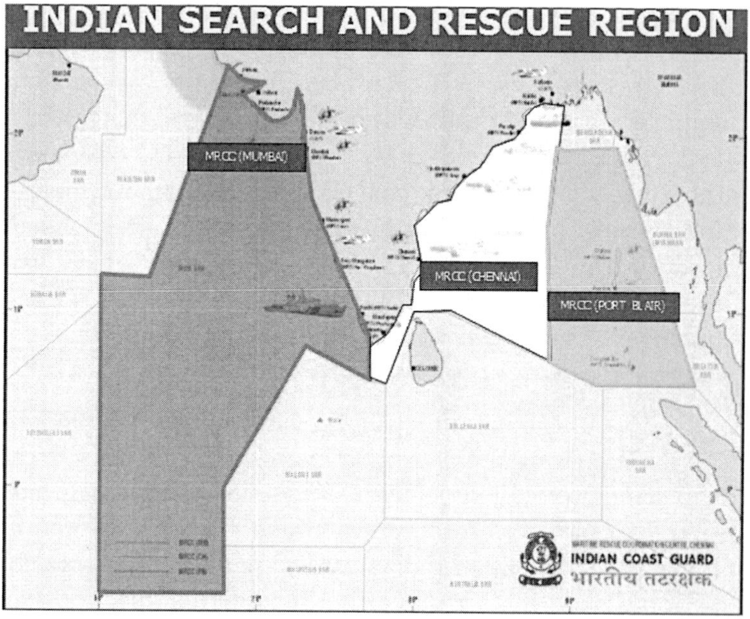

Source: Visit Coast Guard Website, available at <*http://www.indiancoastguard.gov.in/content/447_3_NMSARCA.aspx*>.

Role of Indian Navy and Coast Guard

Taking account of India's geo-strategic location, its size, available mineral, agricultural, human and technological resources, it becomes imperative that New Delhi plays a befitting role in the Indian Ocean region. It will need to strengthen its muscles on all these fronts and its security components. In consonance with its national interests, it will need to strengthen its defence capability. It should be adequate enough to guard its territorial integrity and underpin safeguarding and promoting national interests in the Indian Ocean region.

Since there are no sign of abating maritime issues which

are increasingly posing a serious threat to the peace and security of not only India but also to the region, the role of the Indian Navy and the Coast Guard have to be well prepared both mentally and physically to meet these challenges. The Indian Navy is currently the largest and the most balanced navy in the region and the ongoing modernisation only promises to make it more potent. The naval component of a nation's military strength possesses distinct advantages, not available to the other services. Besides war fighting, the other two roles, viz., policing and diplomacy, form the triad supporting the *raison d'etre* of a nation's navy.[65]

Navies are redefining their roles and also their combat capabilities. While traditional roles remain the *leit motif* of Navies, the altered maritime environment is causing shifts in their conventional responsibilities and functions. The complexity of maritime threats (more from non-state than state actors) and the nature of maritime violence have created a new regime of maritime responses. Navies are increasingly playing a dual role of protecting nations in a traditional strategic sense and enforcing law and order, which includes looking more onshore. Navies are engaged militarily (through the actual use of force – gunboat diplomacy) and politically to enforce a state's maritime security objectives. On balance, the 'cooperative' roles of navies are more visible today than their 'military' roles. Naval cooperation is integral to maritime security which broadly aims at reducing risks of competition and confrontation, minimizing the deployment of naval forces and ensuring a stable maritime security environment – "good order at sea". Naval cooperation is the most preferred, frequent and visible tool of maritime security in the IOR. It was never so in the past. Navies today interact more for non-military purposes for reasons such as to ensure energy, environmental and sea-lane security. Naval cooperation is increasing in proportion to the rising threats to maritime security from non-state actors. There is a new scenario of increased inter-navy interaction today compared to previous periods. Navies of the IOR are interacting with external navies in a friendly fashion.[66]

India has played its role by initiating various CBM's, conducting regular naval exercises and goodwill visits with other regional navies, which have lot to gain from cooperation with Indian Navy which has experience in dealing with transnational crimes and terrorism. India has been spearheading the multinational MILAN exercises since 1995, which is a unique setting comprising 13 navies of Eastern Indian Ocean and East Asia, basically to promote interoperability, build confidence and deal with threats to maritime security. 2014 MILAN Exercises were held in February, AT Port Blair, 16 countries participated in the exercises, highest since its inception. Various bilateral and multilateral exercises involving search and rescue drills, exchange of information and anti terror tactics have been held from time to time by the Indian Navies along with other Navies.

In the coming decades, the challenge of threats such as piracy, gunrunning and drugs smuggling are likely to grow, thus requiring the cooperative use of maritime forces to counter them. Further as majority of the nations in the IOR do not have adequate maritime capabilities to safeguard their interests, they look upon the Indian Navy to ensure stability and tranquility in the maritime domain. The primary task of the Indian Navy towards national security is, therefore, to provide protection from external interference, so that the vital tasks of fostering economic growth and undertaking developmental activities can take place in a secure environment.

Commander Shishir Upadhyaya has noted that two-thirds of the Indian Ocean is under the threat of piracy. He identified challenges such as the size of the surveillance area and reaction time that have hindered navies from capturing pirates, while inadequate legal mechanisms for the trial of pirates has been an issue on land. He suggested that cooperation between navies and the shipping industries and using private security measures would deter pirates.[67]

India's response to maritime security challenges in the Indian Ocean would be to ensure a secure and stable region by engaging the IOR nations and ensuring security of its maritime trade routes. This aspect was covered by the Indian Naval Chief, Admiral D.K. Joshi, in a speech at IDSA on 5 March 2013, where he stated: 'India's geo-strategic location positions us right at the confluence of major arteries of world trade. The Indian Navy is therefore viewed by some of the littorals as a suitable agency to facilitate regional maritime security in the IOR as a net security provider.[68]

During the last three years, the Indian Navy has foiled 39 piracy attacks thereby playing a major role in the ongoing international cooperation against the sea brigands off the African coast. Moreover, since October 2008, Indian warships have ensured the safe passage of over 1,700 ships from around 50 countries through the piracy-infested Gulf of Aden.[69] This year on 10 November, the Indian Navy patrolling the Gulf of Aden foils a multi-boat attack by sea brigands on merchant vessels and capturing 26 pirates. With this, the Indian Navy has successfully conducted five anti-piracy operations. During this operation, the naval personnel on INS Sukanya have captured 14 AK-47 Rifles, 31magazines and 923 rounds of ammunition.[70]

Indian Naval forces are under tremendous pressure to modernise and to upgrade their capabilities to meet contemporary challenges. India with 7516 Km long coastal belt spanning across the nine states and four union territories need to be protected much the same way as the landlocked borders are taken care. To heighten vigil along the Indian coastal stretch, the Indian navy is planning to set up a national command, control, communications and intelligence (C3I) network for maritime domain. Indian navy is also working out a Standard Operating Procedure (SOP) with other stake holders in the maritime domain to avert the possibility of another 26/11. Indian navy is sprucing up its machinery to tackle arms trafficking, smuggling and possible movement of terrorist groups through the Arabian Sea route even as it is required to take on the threat of pirate fishing trawlers and ensuring the safety of oil and gas wells in the waters of Bay of Bengal. Moreover, India's proximity to two strategic commercial straits-Hormuz and Malacca has thrust a greater burden of responsibility on the Indian navy. While more than one third of the international seaborne oil shipments pass through Hormuz, Malacca strait is major sea channel through which a large number of crude oil tankers ply every day.[71]

In the context of the changing maritime dynamics, the Indian navy has taken up significant number of moves aimed at meeting the multiple threats facing India. The Indian navy is looking at drawing inspiration from India's rich maritime tradition to position itself as an ocean-based force multiplier capable of defending Indian interests in all its dimensions. More broadly, there is a range of other initiatives that India might take to engage more constructively in the region and help to enhance regional maritime security and oceans management. The last few decades has witnessed the Indian Navy engaged in an exercise to evolve force architecture to meet the challenges of the 21st century in the Indian Ocean. The Indian Navy is playing an important role to ensure the safety and freedom of seaborne trade against the stronghold of modern-day piracy.

Conclusion

The study found that maritime terrorism, piracy, sea robbery, and poaching is causing grave threat to sea business operation such as sea faring, trading, and fishing along the Indian Ocean. The paper discovers that the operators of these businesses are experiencing coastal insecurity, fear and anxiety due to the criminal activities of pirates. If maritime insecurity breeds threats, then the long term goal has to be to work towards de-securitizing the maritime and building regional maritime security communities. This, in the end, might be the core paradox of current strategies: in order to achieve a desecuritization of the sea in the long run, what is first required is a securitization, that is, the recognition for the serious impact that maritime threats have on economies, livelihoods and national and international security interests.

The counter-piracy network clearly exercises security governance in the Indian Ocean. That it does so, and does so relatively effectively, demonstrates that networks can step in where more formal military cooperation may be impossible. Moreover, it is worth emphasizing the organic nature of the counter-piracy network as a proposed solution to the problems posed by piracy off the coast of Somalia. It was an improvised rather than a planned response that best fit the circumstances at hand. Given this freedom to experiment in order to solve a unique complicated problem, militaries devised innovative solutions that bear little resemblance to cooperation in other areas. Given the difficulties of multinational military cooperation, it is worth considering which features of counter-piracy could be replicated in future multinational military operations.

Although piracy attacks off Somalia may be abating, there is no decline in sea terrorism worldwide. On the contrary, our sea trade routes may never have been more vulnerable and threat to economies through disruption of maritime lines of supply never more relevant. Maritime surveillance is the key to preventing unlawful activities at sea. Maritime security cooperation must encompasses cooperation for the suppression of illegal activity at sea, including piracy, maritime terrorism, drug, arms and human trafficking, and ship-sourced marine pollution; and the provision of relevant safety services, especially search and rescue (SAR) operations; and the mitigation of marine natural hazards.

Piracy can only be addressed by means of a comprehensive multi-layered approach that involves political, technology and societal measures, to strengthen security capabilities, improve intelligence gathering and sharing, and help bring about more effective law enforcement. It also requires multinational cooperation on land and at sea.

References

1. Bojan Mednikarov and Kiril Kolev, "Terrorism on the Sea, Piracy and Maritime Security", Information and Security– An International Journal, Vol. 19, 2006, p. 102.
2. Lydelle Joubert, "The Extent of Maritime Terrorism and Piracy: A Comparative Analysis", Scientia Militaria, South African Journal of Military Studies, Vol. 41, No. 1, 2013, pp. 111-137.
3. Manickam Venkataraman, "Piracy off the Coast of Somalia: Implications for China's Maritime Security", Bandung Journal of Global South, Vol. 3, No. 5, 2016, p. 1.
4. E. R.Lucas, "Somalia's - Pirate Cycle: The Three Phases of Somali Piracy", Journal of Strategic Security, Vol. 6, No. 01, 2013, p. 57.
5. Prashant Kumar and Kaushal Kishor Patel, "India's Response to Somali Piracy: Maintaining the India-Somali Relations", Paper presented in an International Conference in Recent Research Development in Environment, Social Sciences and Humanities, University of Delhi, New Delhi, 27 September 2015.
6. M. Ranstorp and P. Wilkinson, "Terrorism and Political Violence", Terrorism and Political Violence, Vol. 17, 2005.
7. D. Johnson & M. Valencia (eds.), Piracy in Southeast Asia: Status, Issues and Responses (Singapore: Institute of Southeast Asian Studies, 2005).

8. Michael D. Greenberg, et. al. (eds.), Maritime Terrorism: Risk and Liability (Santa Monica, CA: Rand Publications, 2006), p. 10.

9. Andreas Graf, "Countering Piracy and Maritime Terrorism in Southeast Asia and off the Horn of Africa-Applying the lessons learned from the countermeasures against maritime violence in the Strait of Malacca and to the Gulf of Aden", the PiraT-working papers on Maritime Security series, "Piracy and Maritime Terrorism as a Challenge for Maritime Trade Security: Indicators, Perceptions and Options for Actions", project, 5 April, 2011.

10. Ioannis Parinis, "The Maritime Dimension of European Security – Strategies, Initiatives, Synergies", The Fletcher School of Law and Diplomacy Working Paper, No. 1, February 2015, p. 22.

11. Martin N. Murphy, Small Boats, Weak States and Dirty Money (New York: Columbia University Press, 2009).

12. Peter Roell, "Maritime Terrorism – A Threat to World Trade?", in International Relations and Security Network (ISN), Center for Security Studies (CSS) 7 December 2009, ETH Zurich, available at <*http://www.isn.ethz.ch/isn/Digital-Library/Publications/Detail/?id=110282*>.

13. United Nations Convention on the Law of the Sea, 10 December 1982, pp. 60-1, available at <*http://www.un.org/Depts/los/convention_agreements/convention_overview_ convention.htm*>.

14. D. Johnson et. al., "Introduction - Research on Southeast Asian Piracy", in D. Johnson & M. Valencia (eds.), Piracy in Southeast Asia: Status, Issues and Responses (Singapore: Institute of Southeast Asian Studies, 2005).

15. International Maritime Organization (IMO), Assembly 26th session, Resolution A.1025, 18 January 2010, p. 4.

16. International Maritime Bureau – IMB, 'Piracy and Armed Robbery against Ships: Report for the period January 2009–

December 2009', London: International Chamber of Commerce, 2009.

17. Refer to Maritime Terrorism Site, available at *<http://www.maritimeterrorism.com/definitions/>*.

18. Martin N. Murphy, Small Boats, Weak States and Dirty Money (New York: Columbia University Press, 2009).

19. James Kraska and Brian Wilson, "The Pirates of the Gulf of Aden: The Coalition Is the Strategy", Stanford Journal of International Law, Vol. 45, 2009, pp. 243-49.

20. Hans Tino Hansen, "Distinctions in the Finer Shades of Gay: The 'Four Circles Model' for Maritime Security Threat Assessment", in Rupert – Herbert Burns et. al. (eds.), Lloyd's MIU Handbook of Maritime Security (Auerbach Publications Taylor & Francis Group, 2009), p. 76.

21. John Patch, "The Overstated Threat", in M.R. Haberfeld and Agostino Von Hassell (eds.), Modern Piracy and Maritime Terrorism: The Challenge of Piracy for the 21st Century (Dubuque, IA: Kendall Hunt, 2009), pp. 65-75.

22. Rommel C. Banlaoi, "Maritime Security Threats in Post-9/11 Southeast Asia: Regional Responses", in Rupert – Herbert Burns et. al. (eds.), Lloyd's MIU Handbook of Maritime Security (Auerbach Publications Taylor & Francis Group, 2009), p. 254.

23. Christian Bueger, "Learning from Piracy: Lessons for Maritime Security Governance", Global Affairs, Vol. 1, No. 1, 2015.

24. F. Chew, "Piracy, Maritime Terrorism and Regional Interests", Geddes Papers, Australian Defence College, 2005, available at *<www.defence.gov.au/adc/docs/publications2010/Publcns Geddes 2005_310 310_PiracyMaritime.pdf>*.

25. D. Johnson & M. Valencia (eds.), Piracy in Southeast Asia: Status, Issues and Responses (Singapore: Institute of Southeast Asian Studies, 2005).

26. E S Nelson, "Maritime Terrorism and Piracy: Existing and

potential threats", Global Security Studies, Vol. 3, No. 3, Winter 2012.

27. Michael D. Greenberg, et. al. (eds.), Maritime Terrorism: Risk and Liability (Santa Monica, CA: Rand Publications, 2006).

28. Christian Beuger, "Piracy, the Prevention of Maritime Threats and the Lessons from the Contact Group on Piracy off the Coast of Somalia", UAE Counter-Piracy Conference Paper, 'Securing State Recovery: Sustaining Momentum at Sea, Confronting Instability on Land', Organized by the UAE Ministry of Foreign Affairs in Partnership with Global Ports Operator DP World, held in Dubai on 29-30 October 2014.

29. See, '*The National Strategy for Maritime Security*', September 2005, available at *<file:///F:/Piracy/0509%20National %20Strategy%20 for%20Maritime%20Security.pdf>*.

30. Sam Bateman, "Assessing the Threat of Maritime Terrorism: Issues for the Asia-Pacific Region", Security Challenges, Vol. 2, No. 3, October 2006, p. 80.

31. Michael D. Greenberg, et. al. (eds.), Maritime Terrorism: Risk and Liability (Santa Monica, CA: Rand Publications, 2006).

32. Girish Gujar, et. al., "A Strategy for Securing the Maritime Commons", Maritime Insight, Vol. 2, No. 4, Winter 2014, pp. 33-4.

33. Bojan Mednikarov and Kiril Kolev, "Terrorism on the Sea, Piracy and Maritime Security", Information and Security – An International Journal, Vol. 19, 2006, pp. 106-07.

34. P.W. Birnie, "Piracy: Past, Present and Future", in Ellen, E (ed.), Piracy at Sea (Paris: International Chamber of Commerce Publishing, 1989).

35. LMS Peres, "Henrique Galv·o, 1895–1970: Aspects of a Euro-African Crusade". University of South Africa, March 2009, available at *<http://uir.unisa.ac.za/bitstream/handle/10500/3153/ dissertation_peres_.pdf?s equence=1>* and Bojan Mednikarov and Kiril Kolev, "Terrorism on the Sea, Piracy and Maritime Security", Information and Security – An International Journal, Vol. 19, 2006, p. 103.

36. Schiller, TS. "Maritime Terrorism: The Threat", in EF Ellen(ed.), Violence at Sea: A Review of Terrorism, Acts of War and Piracy and Counter Measures to Prevent Terrorism (Paris: International Chamber of Commerce International Maritime Bureau, 1987).
37. M K Bohn, The Achille Lauro Hijacking (Washington, DC: Potomac Books, 2004).
38. Michael D. Greenberg, et. al. (eds.), Maritime Terrorism: Risk and Liability (Santa Monica, CA: Rand Publications, 2006).
39. Schanzer, J. "Yemen's War on Terror". Orbis. Summer 2004, available at *<http://humansecuritygateway.com/documents/WINEP_YemensWarOnTerror.pdf>*
40. M. Richardson, "A Time Bomb for Global Trade: Maritime Related Terrorism in an Age of Weapons of Mass Destruction", Institute of Southeast Asian Studies, Singapore, 2004.
41. RC Banlaoi, "Maritime terrorism in Southeast Asia: The Abu Sayyaf threat", Naval War College Review, Vol. 58, No. 4, Autumn 2005.
42. Michael D. Greenberg, et. al. (eds.), Maritime Terrorism: Risk and Liability (Santa Monica, CA: Rand Publications, 2006).
43. M. Richardson, "A Time Bomb for Global Trade: Maritime Related Terrorism in an Age of Weapons of Mass Destruction", Institute of Southeast Asian Studies, Singapore, 2004.
44. Saloni Salil, "Monsters at Sea: Threat of Maritime Terrorism", Defence and Security Alert, December 2014, pp. 50-1.
45. International Maritime Organization, "Convention for the Suppression of Unlawful Acts against the Safety of Maritime Navigation 1988", 2005, available at *<http://www.imo.org/About/Conventions/ListOfConventions/Pages/SUATreaties.aspx>*.
46. M S McDaniel, "Modern High Seas Piracy", The Law Offices of Countryman & McDaniel, 20 November 2000, available at *<www.cargolaw.com /presentations_pirates.html>*
47. Anna Bowden, "The Economic Costs of Maritime Piracy." One Earth Future and Oceans beyond Piracy, 2010, available

at <*https://www. steamshipmutual.com/Downloads/Piracy/ EconomicCostPiracyOEFReport.pdf*>.

48. Stella Sakellaridou, "Maritime Insurance and Piracy", September 2009, available at <*file:///F:/Piracy/AIDAStellas paper.pdf*>.
49. Martin N Murphy, "Contemporary Piracy and Maritime Terrorism: The Threat to International Security", Adelphi Paper, No. 388, 9 July 2007.
50. R Walker, "Inside Story of a Somali Pirate Attack", BBC News, 2009, available at <*http://news.bbc.co.uk/2/ hi/8080098 .stm*>.
51. International Chamber of Commerce, International Maritime Bureau, "Piracy and armed robbery against ships: Annual report", London, 1 January 2000 – 31 December 2011; International Chamber of Commerce, International Maritime Bureau, "Piracy News and Figures", available at <*www.icc-ccs.org/piracy-reportingcentre/piracynewsafigures*>; International Chamber of Commerce, International Maritime Bureau, "Pirates intensify attacks in New Areas, with first Somali hijacking reported in Red Sea", 18 October 2010, available at <*www.icc-ccs.org/news/315-pirates-intensifyattacks-in-new-areas-with-first-somali-hijacking-reported-in-red-sea*>.
52. International Chamber of Commerce, International Maritime Bureau, "Pirates Intensify Attacks in New Areas, with First Somali Hijacking Reported in Red Sea", 18 October 2010.
53. International Chamber of Commerce, International Maritime Bureau, "Piracy and Armed Robbery against Ships: Annual Report", London, 1 January 2000 – 31 December 2011.
54. International Chamber of Commerce, International Maritime Bureau, Piracy and Armed Robbery against Ships: Annual Report, London, 1 January – 31 December 2012.
55. International Chamber of Commerce, International Maritime Bureau, Piracy and Armed Robbery against Ships: Annual Report, London, 1 January – 31 December 2008.
56. International Chamber of Commerce, International Maritime Bureau, "Piracy and Armed Robbery against Ships: Annual Report", London, 1 January 2000 – 31 December 2011.

57. International Chamber of Commerce, International Maritime Bureau, Piracy and Armed Robbery against Ships: Annual Report, Essex, 1 January – 31 December 2005.

58. UN Security Council, "Report of the Monitoring Group on Somalia Pursuant to Security Council Resolution 1811 (2008), S/2008/769", 20 November 2008, available at <*http://www.securitycouncilreport.org/atf/cf/%7B65BFCF9B-6D27-4E9C8CD3-CF6E4FF96FF9%7D/Somalia%20S2008%20769.pdf*>

59. Prashant Kumar and Kaushal Kishor Patel, "India's Response to Somali Piracy: Maintaining the India-Somali Relations", Paper presented in an International Conference in Recent Research Development in Environment, Social Sciences and Humanities, University of Delhi, New Delhi, 27 September 2015.

60. Rupert Herbert-Burns, "Countering Piracy, Trafficking, and Terrorism: Ensuring Maritime Security in the Indian Ocean", in David Michel and Russell Sticklor (eds.), Indian Ocean Rising: Maritime Security and Policy Challenges (Washington: Stimson, July 2012), pp. 23-39.

61. Christian Beuger, "Piracy, the Prevention of Maritime Threats and the Lessons from the Contact Group on Piracy off the Coast of Somalia", UAE Counter-Piracy Conference Paper, 'Securing State Recovery: Sustaining Momentum at Sea, Confronting Instability on Land', Organized by the UAE Ministry of Foreign Affairs in Partnership with Global Ports Operator DP World, held in Dubai on 29-30 October 2014.

62. Form of Military Cooperation", Journal of Global Security Studies, Vol. 1, No. 4, 2016, p. 270.

63. Swadesh M Rana, "A Template for Those at Risk: India's Response to Maritime Piracy 2010-11", available at <*http://acuns.org/wp-content/uploads/2012/06/Template forthoseat Risk IndiasResponsetoMaritimePiracy.pdf*>.

64. Prashant Kumar and Kaushal Kishor Patel, "India's Response to Somali Piracy: Maintaining the India-Somali Relations", Paper presented in an International Conference in Recent

Research Development in Environment, Social Sciences and Humanities, University of Delhi, New Delhi, 27 Sep. 2015.

65. G S Khurana, "Maritime Security in the Indian Ocean: Convergence Plus Cooperation Equals Resonance", Strategic Analysis, Vol. 28, No. 3, July-September 2004, p. 417.

66. PV Rao, "Indian Ocean Maritime Security Cooperation: Employment of Navies and other Maritime Forces", Centre for Indian Ocean Studies, Osmania University, Hyderabad, India.

67. Shishir Upadhyaya, "Piracy Issues: Current Status and Challenges", Paper presented in a workshop on 'Maritime Security Challenges in the Indian Ocean Region, Jointly organised by National Maritime Foundation and Center for the National Interest, India International Centre, New Delhi, 23-24 February 2011.

68. For the detailed statement, visit Available at <*http://idsa.in/keyspeeches/Role of IndianNavyinMaintaining Peace in Indian Ocean Region_CNS*>.

69. See, "Indian Navy Foils Three Piracy Attempts in Gulf of Aden", available at < *http://www.thehindu.com/news/national/indian-navy-foils-piracy-attempt-in-gulf-of-aden/article2487268.ece*>.

70. See, "Navy Foils another Pirate Attack in Gulf of Aden", Times of India (Pune), 12 November 2011.

71. Radhakrishna Rao, "Meeting Maritime Challenges: Indian Navy Looks Skywards", IPCS Issue Brief, No. 141, February 2010, p. 2.

5

Conclusions and Suggestions

The Indian Ocean is well known as the world's third largest ocean, is of great strategic importance for the supply of crucial energy resources. It provides major sea routes connecting the Atlantic Ocean with the Pacific Ocean. The Indian Ocean is home to critical choke points such as the Bab-el-Mandeb, the Straits of Hormuz, the Straits of Malacca, the Sunda and Lambok Straits. In a world where every nation is dependent on sea for commercial activities and trade, it is necessary to secure these choke points. The disruption of the Sea Lines of Communication (SLOCs) will choke the global economy. With trade concentrated in so few ports in today's global economy, even a single maritime terrorist incident has the potential for significant economic disruptions with considerable financial and human implications. Given these potential impacts, the threat of maritime terrorism must continue to be taken very seriously.

The Indian Ocean is dense with shipping traffic, given that nearly 100,000 ships transit the vast expanse annually through SLOCs. Many of these form the life lines for the littorals as oil tankers and LNG carriers carry energy from the resource rich West Asia to the demand periphery stretching up to NE Asia. Others carry dry/bulk cargo, commodities or containers for trade on which rest the economic indices of these countries. Since most of the trade is sea borne – they are vulnerable to interdiction as nine of the world's most important choke points and narrow passages provide access to this Ocean.

Maritime activity in the Indian Ocean is bound to increase with increased economic activity in this area. The Indian Ocean would continue to remain critical to global trade and food and energy security. The resources of the Ocean increasingly are being exploited by its littoral and island states. It is also a stage for the pursuit of global strategic and regional military and security interests. As the region emerges to become one of the twenty-first century's leading strategic theatres, it will once again be at the crossroads of global trade, economic growth and potential crises. It is a region, in which instability and conflict can quickly arise from imprecise border delineations, internal conflicts, issues of energy and resource security and changing national interests.

The activity in the Indian Ocean region in the coming decades or so will be characterized by extensive trade, energy transfers and a spectrum that ranges from political turbulence on one end, to threats from piracy, terrorism and transnational crime on the other. Indian Ocean's geo strategic and geo-economic importance will rise in the coming decades too. It will continue to remain the lifeline of international trade and links the Atlantic with the Pacific Oceans and critical for global economic prosperity. More recently, natural resources have drawn global maritime communities into the Indian Ocean making it an important international maritime long-haul cargo highway. Nearly half of the world's oil production is transported through the Indian Ocean of which 36 percent comes from the Indian Ocean Region (IOR). More than 80 percent of this oil passes through three Indian

Ocean Straits, namely, Hormuz, Malacca, and Bab-el-Mandeb. Since fossil fuels will continue to supply almost 80 percent of world energy till 2040, the safety and security of International Sea Lanes (ISLs) assumes geostrategic importance.

The Indian Ocean in many ways represents both an opportunity and challenges. The opportunity stems to increase prosperity through increased trade and commerce. The challenge in terms of preserving and protecting our environment and the ocean, that is so much a part of our heritage, is enormous. Maritime security in the IOR in the short-to-medium term is going to be founded upon the robust and sustained naval presence of the larger extra-regional navies and the large regional powers, with the latter group consisting primarily of Australia, Egypt, India, Indonesia, Iran, Israel, Malaysia, Pakistan, Singapore, and Thailand. However, in looking to the longer-term future security of this vital maritime space, the increased naval and/or coast guard capabilities of the smaller forces—such as the Gulf Cooperation Council (GCC) states, Kenya, Tanzania, the Comoros, Madagascar, the Maldives, Mauritius, Mozambique, and the Seychelles-will be crucial in the fight to counter piracy and armed robbery, illicit fishing, and trafficking by sea in high-risk areas.

Maritime security is an issue of fundamental importance for economic growth around the world at the local, regional and global level. The maritime security environment in India's coastline continues to be fragile. Maritime security is an issue of immense relevance as the general paradigm of high sea security is in constant flux. Ensuring stable maritime environment would hold the key to further the economic progress of a country like India and reflects on its global stature and standing among the great powers of the world. Hence, it is necessary that strategically and economically growing nation like India has to keep constant vigil on the operations of its maritime security forces. India has more than five different marine security agencies – is of fundamental necessity. Proper coordination between the Indian Navy, Coast Guard and the marine police forces also holds the key to meeting the maritime challenges facing the country in the twenty-first century.

Maritime security involves a broader concept of piracy and terrorism at sea as well as many other threats to marine navigation. Maritime security risks now also include drug smuggling, human trafficking and threats to marine bio-security, such as the introduction of alien diseases and organisms. Amongst the wide range of threats, terrorism against shipping has become a primary concern, especially since 11 September 2001. Unlike traditional pirates (who are still an active security risk), the perpetrators of terrorist attacks on shipping do not necessarily operate from vessels other than the ships they are attacking. Indeed, their attacks may be to use the targeted ship as the means to deliver a bomb to their selected destination or to employ the ship itself as a weapon. Most important, the perpetrators may not necessarily act with a view to any personal gain for themselves.

With the emerging threats in the Indian Ocean, there emerged a growing awareness that piracy and other organised (maritime) criminal activities are undermining the Indian Ocean's vast resources and its maritime activities. Threats such as piracy and sea-based armed robbery, arms trafficking, human and trafficking, illegal fishing, and dumping of toxic wastes and pollution of the sea threaten to undermine maritime livelihood, travel, trade, and exploitation of resources of the region. These threats engendered a paradigmatic shift in the conceptualisation of threats to the sub-region from land-centred to marine-centred paradigm.

Piracy combines all the qualities of today's transnational security threat: non-state actors engaged in asymmetry attacks, which could potentially cooperate with terrorists, profit from globalisation and legal grey spheres, and other key transnational challenges such as climate-change, ecological degradation and organised crime. That there is the need for a more comprehensive definition of piracy, since UNCLOS's definition limits piracy to unlawful acts of coercion or incarceration carried out on the high seas that does not include similar acts carried out in littoral waters of a state.

Flagging the threat of sea-borne terror and piracy as two key challenges to maritime security and underlining the need to respect freedom of navigation against the backdrop of South China Sea dispute, Indian Prime Minister Narendra Modi declared during the IFR that the Indian Ocean region remains his government's priority given India's 1,200 island territories, and its huge exclusive economic zone of 2.4 million sq km. He further underlined the Indian Ocean region's role "as a strategic bridge with the nations in our immediate and extended maritime neighbourhood." Underlining the need for a "modern and multi-dimensional Navy," Prime Minister Modi stressed that India would continue to actively pursue and promote its geopolitical, strategic, and economic interests on the seas, in particular the Indian Ocean.

India has a great interest in maritime affairs. Prime Minister Narendra Modi declared at the Maritime India Summit in April 2016 that "India has had a glorious maritime future," and is "on the path of shaping an even better maritime future," he was underscoring New Delhi's political resolve to restore India's position of eminence in the global maritime sector. Indian Navy will be playing a crucial role in that endeavour and its strategic vision is in sync with the government's priorities. While changes in the regional and global balance of power remain a significant worry, the bigger problem remains one of introducing organizational changes and doctrinal evolution. How India manages these issues will be significant not only for the Indian Navy's future but also for the rise of India as a credible global military power.

The threat to maritime domain will increase if governments have a lesser interest in addressing maritime terrorism and piracy in the Indian Ocean region. A comprehensive approach to maritime security is indispensable to safeguarding common prosperity and security interests as it effectively protects and supports legitimate activities, while countering the threat of current and emerging terrorist, hostile, illegal or dangerous acts within the maritime domain. By ensuring freedom of navigation and commerce, it also has the capacity to promote regional, and contribute to global, economic stability and protect maritime trade as the heart of regional and global economies.

India maritime strategic interests include energy security, fisheries, mining, and maritime trade to name only a few. Equally vast and varied are the complex maritime security threats and challenges. They span from terrorism and piracy to drug trafficking, gun running, illegal immigration, environmental pollution and movement of contraband. India would therefore need to formulate a comprehensive Maritime strategy that would give her the capability to deter conflict in the region both military and non-military including counter-terrorism and counter-piracy.

Maritime security of India is governed basically by the geography of the Indian Ocean and territories surrounding its borders. India is strategically located in relation to both continental Asia as well as the Indian Ocean region. India's geographical and topographical diversity, especially on its borders, poses unique challenges to our armed forces in terms of both equipment and training. Its peninsular shape provides India a coastline of about 7600 kms and in addition islands in the eastern and western maritime domains of the country. The island territories in the East are 1,300 kms away from the main land, physically much closer to South

East Asia. The Andaman and Nicobar (AN) archipelago is a long chain of islands numbering more than five hundred. They are located astride the Malacca straits, one of the most crucial choke points of IO which is the lifeline for east-west trade and oil transportation. Moreover India's A & N also shares borders with several other littoral countries including Indonesia, Myanmar and Thailand. Therefore, given the strategic geo-political location of the A & N, India has to carefully watch political developments in the region which can surely have implications for the country's maritime security.

Maritime Security is the protection of a nation's territorial and maritime jurisdiction from foreign invasion by sea. It is necessary against military threats from sea. However, today maritime security denotes more than the armed protection provided by a country's navy. Maritime security has acquired a broader holistic meaning. The twenty-first century have witnessed the addition of new and non-military dimensions to maritime security, viz; threats from non-state actors (pirates, drug-traffickers, terrorists), maritime pollution and safety of oil and cargo ships. Relief from natural disasters, exploring sea-bed resources, construction of ports and harbors are also covered by contemporary concept of maritime security.

The growing geo-strategic and geo-economic salience of the IORA makes it evidently clear that there should be greater regional collaboration among the stakeholders to effectively address and confront non-traditional security threats such as maritime terrorism and piracy; trans-national crimes; and environmental & natural disasters. The importance of oceans and seas for trade-led economic prosperity has increased in tandem with growth in the world economy, global merchandise trade and maritime transport activity. However, increased international trade volumes and value have also heightened the exposure and vulnerability of international shipping as a potential target for piracy, armed robbery and other crimes.

Today's transnational threats have the potential to inflict great harm on many nations. Thus, the security of the maritime domain requires comprehensive and cohesive efforts among India and many cooperating nations to protect the common interest in global maritime security. Piracy as a transnational crime has made considerable impact on commercial shipping especially those passing through some of the piracy hotspots in the IOR. Ensuring Maritime Security requires strong and enduring partnerships between civilian and military authorities. This partnership can build on separate initiatives already in place and the respective strengths of relevant actors in the domain of Maritime Security. Enhanced cooperation concerning the Maritime Domain is in the immediate interest of any actor involved in maritime trade and security. Capabilities are either already existent or can be built up in an international co-operative manner. Criminal activities and terrorism could be deterred significantly by concerted action that improves the presence of maritime security forces, enables the boarding of suspicious vessels according to internationally agreed legal rules and provides Maritime Security by Maritime Domain Awareness and integrated civil-military capacities.

The event of 26/11 Mumbai attacks have shaken the entire nation and brought out the need for strengthening coastal security, the government has approved certain important measures for strengthening maritime and coastal security against the threat from the sea. Against the backdrop of multiple agencies involved in coastal security, and the resultant problems of coordination, the Navy has been designated as the authority responsible for maritime security. The government has also decided that it will set up Joint Operation Centres (JOCs) at Mumbai, Visakhapatnam, Kochi and Port Blair under charge of Naval commanders-in-chief. The JOCs will be jointly manned and operated by Navy and Coast Guard with inputs from diverse agencies including Coast Guard, Navy and concerned Central and state agencies.

A national command control communication and intelligence network, for real time maritime domain awareness between the operations rooms of Navy and Coast Guard, both at the field and the apex levels will be established. The Navy will control all Navy and Coast Guard joint operations. This will ensure that the assets are optimally deployed and there is synergy between the two organisations. With these measures, the government expects that a new focus would be given for effectively managing threats from the sea and security for our over 7,500 km long coastline. The Indian Government has also decided to enhance the assets of Navy and Coast Guard by increasing the number of ships, boats, helicopters and aircraft besides manpower. The Navy would also get 80 fast interceptions crafts for sea-front patrolling. The Coast Guard would get a new regional headquarter in Gujarat, which would be designated as north-west region and a new post of Commander Coast Guard to look after surveillance of the state's coast.

Maritime terrorism, gun-running, drug trafficking and piracy are major threats that India is facing from the sea borders of the country. The measures that have been taken and planned to enhance the coastal security include regular aerial surveillance and maritime patrolling along the coast, establishment of coastal police stations in the littoral States, as part of Coastal Security Scheme, vessels monitoring system, etc. All these agencies along with the Coast Guard and the Navy, in the short and long term, prepared, equipped and trained in maritime counter-terror operations to thwart, prevent and deter another terror attack either on the high seas or a Mumbai 26/11 on any other location. Since 2007 Indian intelligence agencies had been issuing warnings of about 500 marine terrorists trained in sea sabotage waiting to enter India by the sea-route. Maritime terrorism requires deep rooted logistic support on land. This is why the, latest terror threat faced by India needs new counter terrorism preparedness. Indian maritime security forces therefore are under constant pressure and challenge to secure the nation's vast coastline from the recurring threats almost on daily basis posed by the illegal and violent forces from the neighbouring and other foreign countries of the IOR. India's coastal security has assumed greater significance in view of the more recent proliferation of violent jihadi fundamentalist groups across the Indian Ocean. Past two decades of Indian experiences sufficiently demonstrated the graver challenges to the national security from the sea by the jihadi groups. But the issue of coastal security figured high on the national security agenda since the November 2008 (26/11) attacks in Mumbai by the Pakistan-backed Lashkar-e-Taiba (LeT), which killed 186 persons. The Mumbai tragedy exposed vulnerability of the India's coastal security. Of particular concern for India is the use of the sea to penetrate and attack India's strategic naval ports which house its important warships, oil resources, infrastructure and high value assets such as atomic and other related plants located near the coast.

Particularly, the timely fusing of maritime information is an initial priority. Incremental improvements in information sharing could allow operational cooperation to develop, as mutual confidence grows correspondingly. For an inter-agency approach to work, the strengths of the relevant organizations involved in addressing Maritime Security must be combined. A better use of the limited resources to address the omnipresent, multinational threat in the maritime domain would produce a most valuable result for governments, international organizations and the commercial sector as well.

Situational Awareness systems have the capability of integrating a wide range of emerging disruptive technologies that include: low cost sensors, IT architecture, video, robotic vision, gaming, 3D/geospatial modeling, physical and virtual augmentation, autonomous systems, simulation software, location-based service, social web life streams, and expert software learning systems. Of course, Situational Awareness platforms will require significant integration to make it useful for users in a networked world. But eventually, it will cultivate our capacity for increased awareness, mindfulness, and focus. It will force learners to expand their collection of inputs, selectively identify their filters used in synthesizing and sense-making, and help to mainstream systems- thinking and underline the imperative of understanding structure, relationships and feedback loops in a globally interdependent world.

The principles of situational awareness based on perception, comprehensiveness and projection might soon support a wide range of applications that reach far beyond military operations and crisis response. It is a user and outcomes-centric systems approach that could integrate anticipated advances in mobility, 'smart' infrastructure, learning systems, policy-making and business intelligence.

Maritime trade is the key to prosperity not only of the Asia-Pacific region, but of the European Union as well. Risks posed by pirates and robberies have already prompted several countries to join forces and pool resources to address the respective consequences. Pooling and sharing between public and private stakeholders could also help address two issues of growing concern.

Maritime security is encountering several other hitherto unnoticed threats to India's coastal security. Recent instances of abandoned ships floating adrift on shores of Mumbai are one such disturbing instances. The piracy emanating from Somalia is another major worry. India needs to strengthen its naval presence along its coastline. There is a need for greater coordination between navy and coast guard. We need to improve our naval presence in the strategic region of Indian Ocean to prevent intrusion of foreign elements.

Maritime security is best achieved by blending public and private maritime security activities on a global scale into a comprehensive, integrated effort that addresses all maritime threats. Maritime security crosses disciplines, builds upon current and future efforts, and depends on scalable layers of security to prevent a single point of failure. Full and complete national and international coordination, cooperation, and intelligence and information sharing among public and private entities are required to protect and secure the maritime domain. Collectively, these five strategic actions achieve the objectives of this Strategy:

a. Enhance International Cooperation

b. Maximize Domain Awareness

c. Embed Security into Commercial Practices

d. Deploy Layered Security

e. Assure Continuity of the Marine Transportation System

Major intra-regional cooperation to encourage capacity-building and to deal with maritime security threats, most significantly terrorism and piracy is urgent. There are enough intra-regional capabilities available which should be leveraged for collective gains.

For many decades, the navies and coast guards of nations have been patrolling territorial and international waters to ensure freedom and protect the vital interests of their maritime borders. Today, when 95 per cent of the world commerce travels by sea and many (both individuals and organized groups) seek to exploit potential weaknesses in national security, the role of traditional maritime forces has changed to a more constabulary nature. There was need to strengthen the Indian Navy as the force had to protect the county from the threat posed by sea pirates and terrorist. Moreover, the navy's role was assuming importance as it had to safeguard the coastal as well as the maritime security. To check and combat effectively the growing maritime challenges, the Coast Guard is closely coordinating its operations like search and rescue, surveillance, hot pursuit, monitoring the maritime jurisdictions and assets, information sharing, etc. closely with the Indian Navy under whose overall authority it has to function.

Indian ability to shape our maritime security environment will require the development of a credible naval presence with adequate assets commensurate with our defence and security interests as well as those required to discharge the role and responsibility expected, of India by the international community. As a diplomatic instrument, the Navy has key attributes- access, mobility, reach and versatility. We need to embed these attributes within the larger vision of India's role in the global arena. A flexible but proactive maritime doctrine is essential to safeguard and project our national interests overseas. The Navy and our foreign policy establishment need to establish closer coordination in this regard. It is too obvious to repeat the statement that India has very significant maritime stakes in the Indian Ocean.

With inherent attributes of mobility, sustenance, preparedness, reach and sealift capability, the Indian Navy is adequately armed to address a broad spectrum of challenges in the Indian Ocean. Its conventional capabilities have undergone a sea change with acquisition of the aircraft carrier Vikramaditya, MiG29K aircraft, and the Chakra nuclear powered attack submarine (SSN); and indigenous construction of Kolkata class destroyers, Talwar and Shivalik class frigates, Kamorta class anti-submarine warfare (ASW) ships, and Sumitra class offshore patrol vessels.

To prevent acts of maritime terrorism from happening, or at least to prevent the worst-case scenarios from happening, a flurry of new maritime security initiatives have been introduced in the wake of 9/11, on both the national and the international levels, such as International Ship & Port Facility Security code (ISPS), Container Security Initiative (CSI), Customs-Trade Partnership Against

Terrorism (C-TPAT), and Proliferation Security Initiative (PSI). On the "business end" of maritime security, both hardware and software solutions are on offer, which can assist maritime law enforcement agencies and port authorities to build up a so-called MDA and defend port facilities against terrorist threats. First of all, the Automated Identification System (AIS) and a satellite-based long-range version named Long-Range Identification and Tracking (LRIT) system provide a more or less detailed picture of what is going on at the high seas (LRIT from December 31, 2008 onward) and near our shores or ports (AIS since December 31, 2004). To further assess a potential threat detected by either AIS or LRIT, several software solutions such as Informa's "Vigilance Vessel Profiling System" have been developed to profile ships with regard to their owners, cargo, previous ports of call, future destinations, and more. On the hardware front, unmanned aerial vehicles (UAVs), sonar systems and sophisticated Closed-Circuit Television (CCTV) supervision systems are available to support port authorities in monitoring their usually vast port facilities.

Right after the 9/11 attacks, the International Maritime Organization (IMO) agreed upon a regulatory framework to address maritime security. The primary concerns identiûed were the need to address the security of vessels and ports, the need to track vessels, the need to ensure the integrity of containerized cargo, and the need to verify and authenticate the identity of seafarers. Security measures aimed at addressing these concerns were adopted and later ratiûed by 108 signatories and made effective on July 1, 2004. In addition to changes to the Safety of Life at Sea (SOLAS) convention, the new international measures include the International Ship and Port Facility Security Code (ISPS), which complements the US Maritime Transportation Security Act (MTSA) by establishing a multilateral security regime containing security-related requirements for member governments together with a series of guidelines on how to meet those requirements.

Indian Ocean's Geo-Strategic Significance

a) The Indian Ocean region is endowed with vast natural resources that remain under-utilised which serve as a source of conflict at the local, regional and global level.

b) The geo-strategic and geo-economic significance of Indian Ocean is inextricably linked to overall development of our country at large.

c) The geo-strategic and geo-economic importance of the Indian Ocean region has grown with the increase of trade and energy flows via international SLOCs.

d) The geostrategic importance of Indian Ocean is accentuated by the fact that, as the most intensively used and strategically important trade highway in the world, it is an intensifying focal point of tensions between the maritime interests.

e) Due to the fact that geo-strategic significance of Indian Ocean will continue to rise in the coming decades or so, there is a need for consensus among the states bordering the Ocean to meet the contemporary and future challenges.

f) The non-traditional issues such as climate change, environmental degradation, resource scarcity and natural disasters will have profound geostrategic implications in the Indian Ocean region.

Indian Ocean's Security and India

a. Emerging maritime security challenges in the Indian Ocean requires special attention.

b. For India, an increasing reliance on imported oil and natural gas to fuel its economic expansion has led the government to view the Indian Ocean as New Delhi's backyard, and as a maritime territory for the Indian navy to dominate and police. India's dependence on the security of the Indian Ocean, combined with its need to monitor and, if necessary, check the naval activity of other powers, means that the country is compelled to reach out deep into the ocean—far beyond its own littoral—to enable more expansive maritime domain awareness.

c. Ensuring stable security in the Indian Ocean area is crucial for global stability and prosperity because it encompasses a vital and expanding intersection of geostrategic rivalries, economic ambitions, resource competition, environmental management, development challenges and demographic change.

d. Since the Indian Ocean region is too vast in its geography, too diverse in the economic needs and priorities of its constituent states, and too disparate in its strategic outlooks to accommodate a 'one size fits all' approach to regional security architecture. The Indian Ocean region's security outlook demands responses that are practical, adaptive and multi-layered. It needs to reflect the realities of major power cooperation and competition, alliance frameworks, sub-regional groupings and more plurilateral arrangements.

e. The safety of the Indian Ocean's SLOCs is of vital importance to the growth of the emerging economies in South and East Asia, as well as the world economy at large. The strategically located choke points are extremely vulnerable to disruptive attacks both from state and non-state actors, including pirates and terrorists. Contingencies at sea have the potential not only to affect already volatile oil prices, but also to have dramatic effects on companies that rely on principle of just-in-time production and delivery within the context of global production networks.

f. Since the competition for access to the resources of the Ocean and seeking to expand their influence will persist, but it should be balanced by promoting and encouraging constructive cooperation among the major powers in the Indian Ocean.

g. Non-traditional maritime security threats are of common concern. However, a common threat perception or prioritisation of issues is lacking, which discourages cooperation between Indian Ocean states. Measures to deal with these threats offer a good rationale for engaging regional partners, so that not only will such cooperation and collaboration help mitigate the impact of threats, but also engender trust and confidence.

h. India cannot remain oblivious to the developments taking place in the Indian Ocean as these have an impact on our progress and prosperity. It should remain vigilant about the developments taking place in the Indian Ocean.

i. Safety and stability of Indian Ocean is the collective responsibility of the regional states. Regional states through resource sharing and as equal partners must cooperate in this regard.

j. In order to effectively move forward in the right direction, and counter the threat of maritime terrorism, it is imperative to simultaneously clamp down on all illegal activities including drug-smuggling, human trafficking and gun running. With the participation of regional countries, execution of the Coalition Maritime Campaign Plan should be ensured.

k. Drugs smuggling, human trafficking, illegal fishing and pollution at sea, are some of the challenges which require the attention of the international community including India. A comprehensive international approach should be adopted to deal with these issues.

l. In order to effectively tackle the threat of maritime terrorism, it became imperative to simultaneously clamp down on illegal activities like drug-smuggling (which constitutes a lucrative source of terrorist funding), and gun running (which keeps the terrorists well stocked in terms of weapons, ammo and explosives).

m. Effective regional legal mechanisms are vital for the good order in the IO. However, such mechanisms are lacking in these seas. Therefore, the littoral states should cooperate in building such mechanisms.

n. For many decades Britain, and more recently the United States have taken responsibility for Indian Ocean sea line protection. Now India, Japan, China and others will have to assess their own growing roles in future SLOC protection.

o. It becomes imperative for India and Japan to closely cooperate to ensure security of the SLOCs and to overcome China's hegemonistic attempts to expand its influence in the Indian Ocean.

Combating Maritime Piracy and Armed Robbery

With regard to combating piracy and armed robbery we propose the following:

a. A first step should be a new look at the Maritime Laws governing the use of force on the high seas and within the territorial coastal areas. These laws need to be taken into the 21st century and adopted to the threats of today.

b. The Rules of Engagement of naval units tasked with protecting the trade routes need to be coordinated and agreed on. Furthermore, a close look needs to be taken at the kind of naval vessels, which might be required to combat piracy more cost effectively.

c. The use of Private Security Companies (PSCs) should be regulated and agreed.

d. Shipping companies need to conform to the basic security requirements when operating in danger areas and should at all times comply with due care for their crew and cargo. They will need to invest in superior passive defense measures and adopt active measures, if required.

e. Police and security services should actively combat those international crime groups involved in piracy at the earliest possible point in time in order to reduce the attractiveness of piracy. They should also prevent piracy from being used by terrorist organizations to advance their aims.

f. The banking community should take a much closer look at money laundering and report all suspicious transactions to the authorities.

g. Long term plans to bring the beginning of stability to Somalia, and the establishment of an effective Coast Guard needs to be drawn up and funding made available. This could be a public-private partnership involving suitably qualified private security companies.

Combating the Threats of Maritime Terrorism

Regarding maritime terrorism, we provide the following recommendations

a. Although we could observe in the last 15 years only a few maritime terrorist attacks, the potential threat should not be underestimated.

b. In spite of recent successes and a decline in successful terrorist attacks by Islamist groups the security services need to continue to keep up the pressure and further improve international cooperation to counter this global threat.

c. The security and intelligence services need to concentrate both on infiltrating the non-Islamist terrorist groups in their relevant countries (HUMINT) and also step-up Open Source Information (OSINT) Research, requiring relevant linguistic and intercultural skills.

d. Governments should consider establishing a National Security Council in their countries, if they have not yet done so, in order to further improve interministerial cooperation and provide a comprehensive security approach.

e. Governments should also consider the harmonized use of Armed Forces within the European Union in the event of major terrorist attacks.

f. Governments should carefully consider their communications policy with the public. Frequent warnings of impending terrorist attacks, which eventually do not materialize, are not helpful in sensitizing the public.

g. Academia can contribute significantly to the activities of the security and intelligence services by helping to analyze the motivation behind fringe terrorist groups and separatist organizations. Such information would be helpful in building up profiles and identifying potential targets of such groups.

h. Businesses should realize that certain terrorist groups present a threat to their business continuity. They should also realize that it is impossible for the state to provide adequate levels of security at all times. Reliable private security organizations are in a position to provide businesses with risk assessment and business continuity plans as well as armed and unarmed close protection.

Appendix – I

External Affairs Minister's address at International Conference on "India and Indian Ocean: Renewing the Maritime Trade and Civilizational Linkages" in Bhubaneswar

Hon'ble Chief Minister of Odisha, Shri. Naveen Patnaik,

Hon'ble Union Minister of State for Petroleum, Shri. Dharmendra Pradhan,

Shri. Sumith Nakandala, Secretary-General, BIMSTEC,

Shri. Tilak De, Chief Post Master,

Shri. Arindam Mukherjee, Secretary, ISCS,

Prof. Sachin Chaturvedi, Director General, RIS,

Excellencies,

Ladies and Gentlemen,

It is with great pleasure that I address you all today at this International Conference, "India and Indian Ocean: Renewing the Maritime Trade and Civilizational Linkages" jointly organized by Research and Information System for Developing Countries (RIS) and Institute of Social and Cultural Studies, Kolkata. I would like to place on record my appreciation for RIS and the Institute of Social and Cultural Studies for their hard work in organizing this

Conference.

The city of Bhubaneswar has a unique distinction of having a rich history which goes back to many millennia and at the same time being among modern India's first planned cities. The city is home to a large number of ancient temples which stand testimony to millennia-old uninterrupted flow of its culture and a number of institutes, or I may say, temples of higher learning. The World Bank has ranked Bhubaneswar as the best place to do business in India. So, it presents an apt location for engaging in deliberations like the one you all are starting today.

The Indian Ocean has been our common maritime home since time immemorial. India was home to some of the earliest seaports in the world and has had a long maritime tradition. The seas around us have facilitated links of commerce, culture, and religion with our extended neighbourhood across several millenniums. This is evident from our cultural footprints which stretch across Asia and Africa.

Importance of the Indian Ocean region from the standpoint of historical and cultural linkages is no less than others.

Ladies and Gentlemen, when it comes to the role of Diaspora we focus on issues where national economic development comes at the centre-stage. When I took over as Minister for External Affairs, I'd an opportunity of participating at the Regional Pravasi Bharatiya Diwas in London, when, along with others, I also rejoiced the success of the Indian Diaspora and invited them to actively participate in India's growth story.

Thanks to our strong community linkages of the Indian Ocean, our respective cultural practices, values and societal ethos are well defined in our folk songs and writings.

Boitha Bandana that is the worshipping of the ships is a practice that has been there since Kalinga days. The ships used to embark on long voyages to Sri Lanka, Bali, Java, Sumatra, Borneo, Malaya, Vietnam and also to China.

While here, if any of you find the time please do visit the Sun Temple of Konarak, where you can see a boat containing a giraffe, which shows linkages with Africa.

The festival of Baliyatra on Karthik Purnima in November is a continuation of this tradition. With commendable efforts of the State government here, this has emerged as a major connect with our ancient maritime legacy.

Small Krathongs or boats on several streets of Bangkok, sometime in November, remind us of Boitha. Similar cultural practices are evident in Indonesia when Mesakapan Ke Tukad is celebrated all across the different islands.

Our writers have captured the movement of people across the Indian Ocean with vivid details. In contemporary times, Amitav Ghosh's 2008 Booker-nominated novel Sea of Poppies captures how a voyage of the East India Company ship Ibis travelling from India to Mauritius has characters from diverse social milieu who recognise themselves as jahaj bhais. It is a saga of the building of nations and the role of migration. It tells us what happens when languages interact. Do we really need a common language to communicate? It is the power of humanity prevailing when Bhojpuri interacts with French to create Creole for building bridges of communication.

Another similar instance comes from another famous writer Shri Giriraj Kishore with his 'Pahla Girmitiya' where he has also explained how individuals responded to the situations they were pushed in. This novel gives a detailed description of how Gandhiji developed his non-violent principles through protest methods like Satyagraha. This year as we celebrate the hundredth anniversary of the return of Mahatma Gandhi to India from South Africa, we salute the courage and conviction with which the `girmitiya' withstood the atrocities and difficult times.

This is an indication of one fact only that we need to reconnect and re-explore these linkages. In his famous poem "The Time Has Come", Lewis Carrol (1872) has a message for us and I recall the few lines by him:

'The sun was shining on the sea,
Shining with all his might:
He did his very best to make
The billows smooth and bright—
'And this was odd because it was
The middle of the night.
The moon was shining sulkily,
Because she thought the sun
Had got no business to be there
'After the day was done—
"It's very rude of him," she said,
"To come and spoil the fun!"
"The time has come," the Walrus said,
The time has come!!'

There is a growing body of evidence to show for example that East Africa had flourishing trade ties with India long before Vasco da Gama discovered the sea route to India via the Cape of Good Hope. Communication between the two regions was facilitated by the monsoon trade winds. India's trade, including spices, cotton and cotton-made fabrics, was reaching countries in far areas of Africa and South-East Asia as well as Europe. India's ancient trade linkages including in the cotton trade with the countries of the Indian Ocean Region and beyond could well be a subject of a standalone in-depth study.

Today, the Indian Ocean carries one-half of world's container shipments, one-third of the bulk cargo traffic and two-thirds of the oil shipments, though three-fourths of this traffic goes to other regions of the world. 90% of our trade by volume and 90 % of our oil imports take place through the sea. We have a long coastline of 7500 km, 1200 islands and 2.4 million square kilometres of Exclusive Economic Zone.

The vast Indian Ocean region hosts over 40 states and nearly 40 % of the world population. It is vast and diverse, home to great cultures and holds immense opportunities for the future.

Therefore, this region which extends from the African coast to West Asia, South Asia and South-East Asia and touches Australia has been a focus of our foreign policy. This is evident from the several visits undertaken by Prime Minister to this region including most recently to Seychelles, Mauritius and Sri Lanka. I myself have also visited most of the countries in this region.

We call this Indian Ocean outreach as 'SAGAR'. As Prime Minister said in Mauritius last week, we seek a future for Indian Ocean that lives up to the name of SAGAR-Security and Growth for All in the Region.

Our vision for the Indian Ocean Region is therefore built on fostering increasing cooperation in our region, use of our capabilities for the benefit of all in our common maritime home and assisting our maritime neighbours and island states in building their maritime security capabilities.

We believe that we will prosper when the seas are safe, secure and free for all. We therefore have advocated collective action and cooperation in the region. We strongly believe that those who live in this region have the primary responsibility for peace, stability and prosperity in the Indian Ocean. At the same time, we recognize that there are other nations, who may have strong interests or presence in the region.

The Indian Ocean has acquired new salience with the shift of the global economic engines to Asia. There has been sustained economic growth in the countries on the littoral of the Indian Ocean. We see growing global stakes and presence in the region. At the same time, the region is witnessing non-traditional threats such as natural disasters, piracy, terrorism, illegal fishing, oil spills and effects of climate change.

Maritime Security is an important dimension of India's bilateral relations with all Indian Ocean Littoral states and through various formal and informal structures currently in place.

We look forward to building closer cooperation in the maritime domain, regularize bilateral maritime exercises and strengthen the dialogues between the navies and the Coast Guards with all littoral countries in the Indian Ocean Region. India is part of various multilateral institutions, which are actively debating maritime security issues in the Asia Pacific region.

The Indian Ocean Naval Symposium, which India founded in 2008, has 35 countries participating in its various activities. The effort has gathered momentum and deepened mutual understanding of maritime challenges and has strengthened our collective ability to address them.

We value our trilateral maritime security cooperation with Sri Lanka and the Maldives. We are exploring possibilities of expanding it to include others in the Indian Ocean Region in particular Seychelles and Mauritius.

The Indian Navy has been playing an important role in this through increased bilateral/multilateral maritime exercises including MILAN which saw participation from 17 regional navies off the Andaman Coast in February 2014.

As a founder member of the Contact Group on Piracy, India has been sensitive to the maritime security situation in the Gulf of Aden for the shipping lanes in this part of the Indian Ocean. Consequently, to protect Indian ships and Indian citizens employed in sea-faring duties, the Indian

Navy commenced anti-piracy patrols in the Gulf of Aden and the sea routes of the Indian Ocean in 2008.

We have been working with like-minded countries to preserve the integrity, inviolability and security of maritime domain which is a global commos. We are committed to maritime security, freedom of navigation, unimpeded lawful commerce and peaceful settlement of disputes in accordance with international law.

We are seeking a more cooperative and integrated future for the region through the overall development of the ocean or blue economy. This would promote increased cooperation in trade, tourism and investment, infrastructure development, marine science and technology, sustainable fisheries and protection of the marine environment.

Through greater collaboration, we look forward to increasing our understanding of marine ecology and resources and improving our abilities to harness new possibilities offered by the Indian Ocean in a sustainable and balanced manner and through a collaborative effort of the countries located in the Indian Ocean region.

In this connection, the Indian Ocean Rim Association for Regional Cooperation (IORARC), which is now known as Indian Ocean Rim Association (IORA) formed in 1997, by Australia, India, Mauritius, Oman, Singapore and South Africa provides an ideal platform. The Association was established with the primary focus on economic cooperation, to promote sustained growth and balanced development of the region and of its Member States, and create common ground for regional economic cooperation.

However, unfortunately, the launching of IORA coincided with the 'Asian Crisis' in 1997, when economically vibrant economies within the region, particularly countries in the East and South-East, were subject to severe economic turmoil and failed to provide adequate support to the new regional initiative. The entire region witnessed a series of external shocks intermittently during the subsequent years. This led to modest progress registered by the Association in its initial phase of little more than a decade. However, significant economic and financial challenges including those flowing from the global economic and financial crisis of 2007 notwithstanding, the members of IORA remained steadfast in their efforts aimed at further consolidating the Association.

At the 11th meeting of the IORA Council of Ministers that took place under India's Chairmanship in Bengaluru in November 2011, the members were unanimous in their approach to identify six priority areas for cooperation in coming years and those are: (i) Maritime Safety and Security; (ii) Trade and Investment Facilitation; (iii) Fisheries Management; (iv) Disaster Risk Reduction; (v) Academic and S&T Cooperation; and (vi) Tourism Promotion and Cultural Exchanges.

The visibility of the grouping has increased in recent years with the initiation of several new activities in different cooperation mechanisms under IORA. Member countries have shown renewed interest in participating and also in launching a number of programmes to coordinate between regional economies in a diverse range of areas including capacity building, scholarships programmes, among others.

On the economic front, IORA exhibited significant dynamism in the past few years. The region experienced steady growth in global and intra-regional trade since 2003. Global trade expanded by 3.5 times from USD 1,224 billion in 2003 to USD 4,232 billion in 2012 whereas intra-regional trade increased by more than four times from USD 302 billion to USD 1,230 billion over the same period. Intra-regional trade ratio that measures the degree of trade integration in the region has also registered a significant increase over the years. This growth in intra-regional trade without any formal trade arrangement among the member states reflects the potential existing in the region for deepening regional economic integration.

Besides goods, the region witnessed a significant rise in services trade. The region as a whole was found competitive in services sectors such as telecommunications, computer and information services; transport and travel whereas individual member countries are competing in a number of other services sectors also.

However, the full potential of intra-regional trade remains untapped because of poor communication and transport links, lack of information about the supply capabilities, among other barriers. The ports in most of the region need to be modernized and equipped with multi-modal transport facilities besides efficiency improvements. The customs and clearance procedures at borders need to be streamlined to reduce delays and costs of transit.

Similarly, the intra-regional investment is still negligible despite tremendous potential. Deepening of regional economic integration may help in exploiting this hidden potential of intra-regional cooperation for mutual benefit.

The existing trade potential can be further tapped through sectoral cooperation initiatives. The emerging sectors that present immense potential for trade expansion and regional integration include food processing, fisheries, tourism, environmentally sensitive goods, information technology, SMEs, regional value chain, and so on. Time has come that the countries in the region consider evolving a common regional standard to promote intra-regional trade. Some mechanisms need to be evolved to address the challenges and hindrances in the way of trade growth to ensure that intra-regional trade becomes significant to make the overall economic performance of IORA vibrant.

We see IORA is as a regional body that can respond effectively to the needs and enhance individual and collective capacities of Member-States to tackle contemporary challenges of sustainable and balanced economic growth, development and common maritime domain. The IORA provides an effective multilateral platform that facilitates the realization of untapped opportunities for prosperity, peace and development of the region. The growing number of membership and the number of Dialogue Partners is a testimony of growing salience of the Indian Ocean and IORA as the apex body in the Region.

It gives me satisfaction to note that IORA members are taking a number of initiatives to address the challenges in the way of further deepening of trade and economic ties amongst themselves.

I am sure this Conference would facilitate the exchange of ideas, concerns and experiences of IORA Member States and would help evolve a common understanding to address the emerging challenges in the region. I look forward to substantive and fruitful discussions ahead.

Once again I thank RIS and the Institute of Social and Cultural Studies for their timely initiative to organize this conference and inviting me to share my vision with the galaxy of scholars and experts present here.

Thank you.

March 20, 2015

Appendix – II

Statement by External Affairs Minister at the 12th Council of Ministers' Meeting of the Indian Ocean Rim Association for Regional Cooperation (IOR-ARC)

Excellencies,

Ladies and Gentlemen,

We are meeting today at an important juncture. We launched IORARC in 1997, a decade and a half ago, with the primary objective of promoting sustained growth and balanced development of the region and its Member States. IORARC has helped promote understanding and cooperation amongst our countries over these years, yet immense untapped potential remains.

The geo-strategic importance of the Indian Ocean cannot be underestimated. As the focus of global economic growth shifts to Asia, it will occupy even greater salience in our strategic perspective. We envision IORARC as a regional body that can respond effectively to this need and enhance our individual and collective capacities to deal with contemporary challenges facing our common maritime domain. It must be strengthened to enable it to rise to our expectations.

We considered it appropriate, therefore, to focus our deliberations today on the theme "IORARC at 15 – the Next Decade". In our view, the objective of this exercise should be to lay down a roadmap and agenda for our Association for the coming years that will eventually establish IORARC as an apex organization for the Indian Ocean region.

Our region is characterized by great diversities in size, population and levels of development. A prospective roadmap for our Association must therefore be inclusive, taking IORARC forward at a pace acceptable to all.

Secondly, in facilitating the creation of a regional climate conducive to peace and prosperity, IORARC should aim at opening as many channels of communication and cooperation amongst its membership as feasible. It must thus be comprehensive, an integrated effort bringing together governments, civil society and business and deepening people-to-people contacts.

In this context, we should consider a university dedicated to a comprehensive range of subjects relevant to the Indian Ocean including its political economy, maritime and environmental issues.

And finally, its agenda must reflect common regional interests that hold value for its membership. We took the first steps when we last met in Bengaluru in November 2011, and identified six priorities for our Association's work, including maritime security and safety, disaster risk reduction, trade & investment facilitation, fisheries management, academic and S&T cooperation, and tourism and cultural exchanges.

Each of these areas has its own relevance for us. Here I would like to touch on just three aspects.

Economic cooperation is at the core of our collective

effort, and we need to consider appropriate initiatives aimed at meeting the developmental, energy and food security needs of our region, new infrastructural linkages with enhanced connectivity, and trade and investment facilitation that builds on the complementarities in our economic strengths.

Job creation for our growing youthful populations is imperative across our region. Capacity building and skilling in all our identified priority areas is a cross-cutting need, which IORARC can also address.

Economic development cooperation requires a conducive environment to flower. Security of maritime commerce and safety of seafarers are of concern to all of us. There is a need, for example, to be more precise in defining High-Risk Areas in the Indian Ocean, based on actual incidents of piracy, as this impacts adversely on insurance premiums and adds to the cost of shipping in our region. India will host an IORARC seminar on maritime security in early 2013, and we should consider its institutionalization as a regional forum for continuing exchange of views and monitoring of the situation.

Finally, we should consider ways and means of providing greater structure to the IORARC process. We could consider having a theme of contemporary relevance for future Council meetings, for example, as we have done for this one, which can help focus our discussions on the issues at hand.

Excellencies, I thank you for your attention and look forward to hearing your views.

Gurgaon,

November 2, 2012

Appendix - III

Speech by Foreign Secretary at National Maritime Foundation on "India as a Consensual Stakeholder in the Indian Ocean: Policy Contours"

Admiral Arun Prakash, Chairman NMF

Commodore C Udai Bhaskar, Director NMF

Ladies and Gentleman

It is indeed a privilege for me to speak at the National Maritime Foundation which has made an invaluable contribution to raising maritime awareness and in promoting the concept of 'Maritime India'- a task that Sardar KM Pannikar, India's foremost naval historian, would have warmly applauded. I congratulate Admiral Arun Prakash and his team at the Foundation for their efforts. I thank them for the invitation to speak here today.

India and the Indian Ocean are inseparable. In the midst of the third largest ocean in the world, India's location is in many ways her destiny. That is not just a statement regarding a fact of geography but of deeper civilizational, historical, cultural, economic and political linkages that have been forged between India and the Ocean that bears its name. Throughout history, India's wellbeing and prosperity was linked to its access to the Indian Ocean region. It is no coincidence that the decolonization of the littoral countries of the Indian Ocean region was catalyzed by India's independence and emergence as a free nation. The Indian diaspora is a prominent presence in almost all countries of the region. Apart from the Monsoon, the India-link, in its broadest sense, is the single common thread that is visible in the Indian Ocean region.

The organic unity of the Indian Ocean was fractured during the colonial period. Now, the winds of globalization are bringing a fresh bond of unity in the Indian Ocean region. Globalization is inseparable from its maritime dimension, as 90 % of global trade by weight and volume is carried by sea. India is a major stakeholder and beneficiary of globalization. As an emerging global economic and trading power, India has thus a vital stake in maritime security. India's global mercantile trade has grown phenomenally and now constitutes 41% of our GDP. 77% of our trade by value and over 90% by volume is carried by sea. India is now projected to become the fourth-largest economy in the world by 2020, after China, Japan and the US. Our dependence on seaborne trade is expected to expand exponentially. The maritime dimension is also vital for our energy security. India's oil consumption is expected to rise to 245 million tons annually by 2020, with the country likely to be the world's single largest importer of oil by 2050. Our economic growth would continue to be critically depended upon the unhindered flow of oil. The Indian Ocean region is important for India in terms of trade and as a source of energy supplies. Trade with the littoral states of the Indian Ocean constitutes close to 40% of India's total trade.

The Indian Ocean is virtually land-locked. It is distinguished by a land rim on three sides; Asia to its north, Africa to its west and SE Asia and Australia to its East.

Access to the region is only possible through seven established gateways or choke points. To the East, the Straits of Malacca, Sunda and Lombok connect the South China Sea to the Indian Ocean. The congestion and the narrow width of these straits make them susceptible to possible terrorist attacks. The Malacca Straits are the primary route, through which more than 50,000 vessels transit annually. To the west, the world's busiest shipping lanes pass through the Strait of Hormuz, which connects the Persian Gulf to the Indian Ocean. The Malacca Straits handle 40 % of world trade; the Straits of Hormuz handle 40 % of all traded crude oil. It is not hard to imagine the consequences to the global economy if these chokepoints are indeed choked. The Indian Ocean is also one of the world's most important waterways, with 50% of the container traffic and more than 70% of crude and oil products being carried through it. The disruption of energy flows in particular is a considerable security concern for littoral states, as a majority of their energy lifelines are sea-based. The world thus has a vital stake in the stability of the archipelagic countries. It's not just the use of waterways that is important, but access to them as well. Landlocked countries are now, therefore, gaining a new geopolitical significance, for transit roads and pipelines.

It is now a widely accepted truism that the geopolitics of the Indian Ocean region is a microcosm of global geopolitical trends. There are countries which are developing rapidly; on the other hand, there are those which are on the brink of collapse. In between, there are those which are emerging from conflict and show promise of making rapid strides in the future. There are a large number of democracies in the region but it cannot be said that democracy is a universal norm for the region. A number of countries suffer from weak governance and regime instability, vulnerable to non-state actors driven by extremist ideologies. Threats to stability in the region abound, ranging from terrorism, piracy, warlordism, proliferation, smuggling and drug trafficking. The situation off the Horn of Africa is a source of particular concern. The situation in land-locked Afghanistan also impacts on the Indian Ocean region, as a substantial portion of the international military presence there is dependent on support from maritime assets and capabilities. The impact of climate change is of concern to several island states that face a threat to their very survival. But, the bright side is that parts of the Indian Ocean littoral are witnessing an unprecedented economic boom, driven by positive economic and demographic factors. The overall picture is therefore mixed and complicated, not lending itself to easy categorization or solutions. What is certain is that India stands out both in what it has achieved and the untapped potential that still lies ahead. In short, the future of the Indian Ocean region is unthinkable without India.

By any objective criteria, India has very significant maritime stakes in the Indian Ocean. We have a coastline of over 7500 km. Between the Lashwadeep and the Andaman and Nicobar chains, we have over 600 islands, with the southernmost tip just 90 nautical miles from Indonesia and the northernmost tip less than 10 nautical miles from Myanmar. In terms of maritime security terms, these are significant assets. Our EEZ is more than 2.5 million square KMs. The mining areas of over 150,000 sq KMs allotted to India under UNCLOS are about 2000 km from our southernmost tip. We have significant interests in Antarctica as well. For several decades, India was the only Asian country to possess an aircraft carrier. Our naval force posture in the coming years will require the necessary capabilities in terms of reach, sustaining power and sea control. Following the sea-borne terrorist attacks on 26/11 in Mumbai, concerted efforts have been undertaken for strengthening maritime and coastal security against threats from the sea, with greater involvement of the Navy, the Coast Guard and all the coastal states.

As India's development is predicated on a stable geostrategic environment, as a mature and responsible nation, it is in our interest that we play an active role in the architecture of maritime security based on the twin principles of shared security and shared prosperity. India is well poised to play a leadership role in this regard. We have friendly and productive bilateral relations with almost all the states in the Indian Ocean region. Our bilateral relations with Sri Lanka, Bangladesh, Indonesia, Mauritius, Maldives, Seychelles, Oman, Madagascar, Kenya and others give us unprecedented access to a wide swathe of the Indian Ocean. Some of these are territorial neighbours but all are maritime neighbours. We have historical and civilisational ties with many of these countries. Some of these countries have large Indian communities. The broad spectrum of our ties with these countries has a strong economic and socio-cultural dimension. Maritime security thus gives us a new perspective on our bilateral relations with these countries. We are actively engaged with almost all regional bodies that are either based in or border the Indian Ocean region- ranging from SAARC, BIMSTEC, ARF, ASEAN, GCC, SADC to the AU. We are interested in building a web of cooperative relations that brings together all the stakeholders based on mutual interest and benefit. Our 'soft power' gives us advantages that few other countries can match in this region. There is almost universal acceptance of India's credentials and recognition of the vital contribution that we can make for the stability and prosperity of the entire region.

Our economic growth acts as a driver for growth across the entire region. Our bilateral and multilateral assistance programmes are crucial for the security and development requirements of a number of countries. Drawing on its human resources and scientific expertise, India has been assisting traditionally in areas such as agriculture, health, education and IT, as also in capacity building in areas such as hydrography, oceanography, dealing with climate change, etc. It is true that optimizing our economic and technical assistance programmes, even while integrating them with our larger security and strategic interests would yield even greater benefits. This will require leveraging India's soft power and technological strengths as also ensuring greater synergy amongst the various instruments that we can deploy - diplomacy, trade and economic factors and military assistance.

We are proud of the fact that our Navy has emerged as a versatile and flexible diplomatic instrument to mark India's presence in the region. The Ministry of External Affairs and the Navy have partnered together as maritime diplomats. There is hardly a port in the region where our ships are not welcome. We have the distinction of undertaking naval exercises in the Indian Ocean with all the major navies of the world. The prompt assistance provided by the Navy in the aftermath of the Indian Ocean Tsunami was an eye-opener with regard to our capabilities for providing timely disaster relief and humanitarian assistance. The Navy did a commendable job in helping in the evacuation of over 2280 people from strife-torn Lebanon under Operation Sukoon. The Indian Ocean Naval Symposium (IONS) initiative, launched by Indian Navy has provided a forward-looking framework for constructive engagement among the navies of the region. This initiative has tremendous potential as an inclusive forum for all stakeholders, which have legitimate interests in the region. Under the ARF, India has contributed to discussions on maritime security. India has also contributed to regional efforts for safe navigation in the Malacca straits.

While India is seen as a net security provider, we cannot carry the burden of regional security on our shoulders alone. No doubt maintaining a favourable maritime balance will require the development of a credible naval presence with adequate assets commensurate with our defence and security interests as well as those required to discharge the role and responsibility expected of India by the international community. The era of gunboat diplomacy is long over. A robust Indian naval presence is seen as a necessary contribution to a cooperative regional security order. The cooperative burden-sharing of naval forces to fight piracy off the coast of Somalia is a case in point. Our navy has discharged its responsibilities with distinction and is viewed as an indispensable partner not just by regional states but by the UN, EU and NATO naval forces. India is engaged with other countries on capacity-building and consultations in the area of anti-piracy to devise measures for keeping open access points to avoid choking international trade. While we are addressing the immediate threats to maritime security, the international community must find ways of dealing with the failed or failing states where violence and institutional fragility are being exploited by non-State actors and others which have a presence of international terrorist groups on the Indian Ocean littoral which in fact radiate instability in the region as a whole. The recent global financial and economic crisis has aggravated the fragility of many littoral States, some of which are among LDCs.

While addressing the threats posed by non-state actors is important, we would also require states themselves to abide by "rules of the road." Maintaining free access to the sea is very much part of defending the 'Global Commons'. This will require a common vision of maritime security and freedom of navigation in accordance with universally agreed principles of international law and peaceful settlement of maritime territorial disputes. The maritime balance in the Indian Ocean region is linked to developments in South East Asia, the Pacific Rim and the Mediterranean. It is unrealistic to presume that we would be able to insulate our region from instability elsewhere. Maritime Security cannot be sustained if there is an exclusive focus on the military dimension alone, for it has economic, political and social dimensions as well. It is also unrealistic to expect that any single power can presume for itself the role of a "sea-based balancer". Lastly, cooperation on maritime security issues could provide the necessary trust and confidence to build a flexible and adaptable Pan Asian Security Order.

A popular theme in the media is to project the Indian Ocean as the new theatre of big power conflict. A widely read analyst who has also published a book on the Indian Ocean recently spoke of India being a "global pivot state supreme", in the so-called tussle between the United States and China. While this description is flattering, we do not make policy on the basis of 'feel-good labels'. There is no inevitability of conflict. India views the emerging trends with realism-building sustainable regional security will require a cooperative effort among all regional countries on the one hand and all users of the Indian Ocean. As the main resident power in the Indian Ocean region, we have a vital stake in the evolution of stable, open, inclusive and balanced security and cooperation architecture in the region. By definition, this would need to be a consensus-based process, where all the stakeholders who have a legitimate presence in the region make their respective contributions to regional security. India stands for harnessing the forces of geo-politics for new forms of cooperation rather than it being used as an excuse for domination by any single country. That is the vision that we aspire to. And that is the vision we look forward to realizing our partnership with all countries of the Indian Ocean region.

Before I conclude, let me briefly speak about the Indian Ocean Rim – Association for Regional Cooperation (IOR-ARC) that came into existence in 1997. India was one of the 14 founding member States. Given the growing strategic significance of the Indian Ocean, this organisation is the only one which aims to create a web of cooperative relationships between the now 18 member countries spanning three continents and three water bodies: this provides the right balance in terms of developing the littoral countries, across the political and geopolitical spectrum, in a direction where economic, trade, academic and cultural cooperation constitutes the core of these relationships. The political and the strategic subtext of this organisation's activities are very relevant in the current times. Although the organization has not been able to fulfil its stated potential as yet, it does provide us with a useful platform to articulate our inclusive non-polarising vision of the future of the Indian Ocean and its littoral.

Let me conclude by commending the Maritime Foundation for their valuable contribution to the national discourse on maritime issues.

Thank you.

New Delhi

November 19, 2010

Index